THE
DYNAMICS
OF
GRIEF

THE
DYNAMICS
OF
GRIEF

David K. Switzer

ABINGDON PRESS ⑤ *Nashville and New York*

THE DYNAMICS OF GRIEF

Copyright © 1970 by Abingdon Press

ISBN 0-687-11313-X

Library of Congress Catalog Card Number: 74-112333

The scripture quotation noted NEB is from
the New English Bible, New Testament. ©
the Delegates of the Oxford University Press
and the Syndics of the Cambridge University
Press 1961. Reprinted by permission.

SET UP, PRINTED, AND BOUND BY THE
PARTHENON PRESS, AT NASHVILLE,
TENNESSEE, UNITED STATES OF AMERICA

foreword

Forewords are what most readers of most books can do without. Therefore, my first decision was to omit the presumably superfluous page. But then my own needs came more alive and cried out and pushed for expression. The needs of the author become the rationale for these few lines. It would simply be thoughtless, indeed, impossible for me not to convey in print something of my indebtedness to others for their major role in the process of which this book is the recording of one stage.

Dr. David Eitzen, at the time Professor of Psychology of Religion at the School of Theology at Claremont California, provided the discussion group context out of which came the initial impetus to put into written form some of the ideas and experiences which had become a part of me but which were yet unclearly formulated and unorganized. From the time the first written form was achieved, two persons continued to urge me to submit the material for publication, Dr. Howard Cline-bell, Professor of Pastoral Counseling at the School of Theology at Claremont, and my wife, Shirley. Without their encouragement and persistence I am sure that I would never have undertaken such a project.

How can I possibly recognize in an appropriate way those many persons with whom I have shared the intimate and intense experience of grief as I have sought to be of some usefulness to them in their time of distress, but who, in allowing me to enter into their lives at such a time, gave so much to me? They know who they are, and if they should happen to read this, I would say, "I express to you a gratitude of which you are probably not aware, for I continue to remember, just as you do, this painful, meaningful time together. You and those whom you have mourned have become a part of me."

contents

1

The Paradox of Grief:
Its Universality and Its Neglect

"I've been such a fool. I thought she would always be here."
A man in his sixties was expressing in the midst of his an-
guished sobbing following the death of his wife the self-
chosen delusion with which most of us seek to protect ourselves from one of the most obvious realities of life. We tend
to live as if we would never experience the jarring separation by death from those persons with whom we have closely
linked our lives.

Many people live many years before being brought hard up

against this devastating event. Others are caught up by the power of its emotion very early in life. But no one escapes. Depending upon many circumstances, the form and intensity of the reaction to the death of someone who has played an important role in one's own life may vary. However, where the emotional relationship has been close, the impact of the death makes itself felt and its influence remains with a person for the rest of his life. He can never again be as if the loss had not taken place.

Even the small child who is not consciously able to comprehend what has happened when a parent dies has certain characteristic responses to the event. Older children, having some degree of understanding but without some of the qualities of adult relationships, are also touched in unique ways. A nine-year-old boy had been deeply affected by the death of a close friend at school. There were not the tears and sobs and an awareness of other feelings which most adults might have experienced, but his own being was just as shaken, just as threatened, and the questions which he raised were in their own way as profound as those of any older person.

A seminary student wrote in a paper:

Death is undoubtedly the loneliest experience that a person will ever have during the time he lives on earth, where he is the only one who can experience it at the time. It was at an early age that I first realized that people actually stopped living. My first response to such an event was to question why people die.

As a teen-ager, I experienced one of the most penetrating events in my life thus far. The event was the death of my third youngest brother. It was from this point that I began to look seriously at this thing called death. During the funeral of the younger brother, I was perplexed over the reasoning for his death. I did not really understand what the minister was saying.

All that I could understand was something about God knowing the reason for his death. This did not go well with me at all. In fact, it made me angry because I wanted to know the reason for his death. My situation was even more difficult to bear because I thought that a person was not supposed to cry, especially a male, so I held my emotions inside.

Time has cooled my anger, but time has not deadened my quest for understanding the reason for death, and even more important, to learn to bear grief successfully. As I became a minister, I also received requests to hold funerals. The words said at the first funeral that I held were well-worn conservative clichés. I only hope that they meant something to someone and helped them to deal with their grief, because they meant little to me.

Considering the power of such an experience as the death of an emotionally related person, considering its universality, considering the fact that most persons as family members and friends and many professional people in the performance of their professional roles are called upon to minister to the person in grief, remarkably little has been written on this topic with the purpose of clarifying precisely the inner dynamics of it. Why do people have the feelings they do in response to the death of someone close to them? Why is it that an event external to oneself produces such pain within, such feelings of emptiness, meaninglessness, fear, and depression? How may a person deal most effectively with his own grief and how may he relate himself most helpfully to others who mourn?

DEFINING GRIEF

Even though a number of books and articles have dealt with the subject of grief, the need for a clear definition still remains. As one reads the literature, he notices that the word "grief" has been used to apply to the behavioral reactions of the bereaved person in two ways. First, it has been referred to as if it were a separate emotion with its own unique set of characteristics, but without stating clearly what it is if it is different from other emotions, except for the obvious reference to the external stimulus of death which cues it off. On other occasions it has apparently been used to refer to the complex combination of several different emotions which are expressed at the time of the death of a significant other person.

Not only has the word "grief" been used in these different ways, but there has also been some confusion between it and the word "bereavement." Technically grief and bereavement are slightly different, bereavement being the actual state of deprivation or loss, and grief being the response of emotional pain (including, as the use of the word "emotional" always should, certain physiological accompaniments) to the deprivation.

Because of the lack of consistent usage of the term "grief," it has had for many relatively little precise meaning. To correct this lack of clarity and precision is one of the aims of this book.

It should be recognized from the outset that significant losses of persons may take place in ways other than death: divorce, extended separation related to business or military assignment, children growing up and leaving home, etc. In addition, similar emotional reactions take place in other situations involving the loss or threatened loss of things or even a status that a person perceives as important to his life: the loss of one's job or business, a demotion in position, a failure in school, the destruction of one's home and possessions by fire. In this book the emphasis will be upon loss by death. The most concise expression of the thesis is that grief has as its core experience an acute attack of anxiety, precipitated by the external event of the death of a person with whom one is emotionally involved, and that other behavioral responses are dynamically related to the anxiety. Several different approaches to a definition of anxiety will be shown to be involved in the reactions that are noted in the grief situation. To clarify this view, normal grief will be investigated in the light of the relation between the death of an emotionally significant person and the personality structure and dynamics of the bereaved person.

THE NEGLECT OF GRIEF

In the light of the universality of grief and its impact in human life, it is particularly surprising that the field of psychology, "the science of human behavior," has largely ignored this powerful human emotion. A rather thorough search of books dealing with the development and functioning of personality, the psychology of personal adjustment, and those discussing emotions specifically, reveals that grief is usually mentioned not at all, or else it is referred to only briefly and usually somewhat superficially. It is interesting, and not wholly unrelated to our purposes here, to seek the reason for such a serious omission in psychological literature. To be sure, a part of the reason may be the fondness of psychologists for experimental procedures. Clearly, the grief situation does not readily lend itself to experimental manipulation, nor even to the usual forms of controlled observation. The situation is simply too sensitive to be intruded upon by a methodology which in any way would make a person's reactions more painful.

However, the real reasons may lie in another area; namely,

13

the tendency of all of us to withdraw from a serious contemplation of death and the painful memories and emotions which surround it. Feifel relates the resistance he encountered when he sought to investigate persons' ideas and feelings concerning their own impending death by interviewing terminal hospital cases. The resistance, interestingly enough, was not from the patients themselves, but from hospital administrative officers and staff members. He concluded that "death is a taboo subject in the United States, surrounded by disapproval and shame."[1] If a discipline makes the claim that it studies human behavior, one would expect that it would include all human experiences in its investigations. If it does not, there must be some reason. Psychology has collected very little data about experiences surrounding death. Feifel feels that this reflects the fact that "scientists and professional people are no less immune to prejudice [concerning death] than other groups, not only other disciplines, but psychological colleagues as well."[2] He summarizes the problems surrounding the investigation of death, and this would seem to hold true for using as subjects those who have recently had an emotionally significant person die as well as patients who are confronting their own impending death:

One's own willingness to face or avoid the thought of death can be a relevant variable in the ensuing data. Few undertakings in psychological research, I think, are more emotionally exacting. Pain and death are not themes comfortably encompassed by categories of methodological rigor and theoretical relevance. Not only is the emotional resistance to the investigator . . . but so also is the potential emotional scotoma of the researcher himself. The investigator is confronted with the Scylla of being affectively

[1] Herman Feifel, "Death," *Taboo Topics,* ed. Norman L. Farberow (New York: Atherton Press, 1943), p. 14.
[2] *Ibid.,* p. 15.

swamped, reactivation of his own anxieties about dying, antipathy toward or overidentification with certain kinds of [persons] . . . and the Charybdis of overintellectualizing his approach, dissembling behind a façade of pseudorigorousness, and refusing to observe any but the grossest and least emotionally tinged dimensions of what is happening. Research on human behavior in extreme situations asks for a delicate balance of identification and intellectual detachment (Wallace, 1956).[3]

Wahl has also been aware of the paucity of psychiatric investigation on the subject. The lengths to which people go in their attempt to deny and distort the reality of death because of their powerlessness to cope with it has led even the professionals in the area of human behavior to seek evasive tactics.

Psychiatry, by the very nature of its field, has always been concerned with the investigation and elucidation of those aspects of human character and symptom formation which the average man is prone to shun. And yet it is a surprising and significant fact that the phenomenon of the fear of death, or specific anxiety about it (thanatophobia), while certainly no clinical rarity, has almost no description in the psychiatric or psychoanalytic literature.[4]

An operational definition of grief which grows out of or contributes to the methods and procedures of investigation has not yet been clearly stated. Nor have the mere descriptions of the behavior of grief by themselves been an adequate substitute for such a definition that would lead one to a more thorough understanding of the dynamics at work in the reaction.

[3] *Ibid.,* p. 13. Feifel's reference is to A. C. Wallace, *Human Behavior in Extreme Situations* (Washington, D. C.: National Academy of Sciences, 1956).
[4] C. W. Wahl, "The Fear of Death," *Bulletin of the Menninger Clinic,* XXII (1958), 215.

Psychoanalysis has been considerably more productive in its observations and writings on the subject of grief than has psychology. Nevertheless, though many valuable insights are presented, there seem to be at least two shortcomings. First, most of the articles do not seek to investigate and define grief as such, grief being incidental to other concerns. Second, most of the investigations deal with the pathological manifestations of grief. The nature of the work of the psychotherapist does not bring him into frequent contact with grief in its usual expressions. A majority of cases reported have been those persons already undergoing therapy who, while in this process, also experience bereavement.

Since the person in our society who is regularly brought in contact with persons experiencing grief in its normal expressions and whose major function is to operate in the situation to facilitate mourning is the clergyman, it is not surprising that a larger amount of literature dealing with grief comes from this source. Most of it, however, approaches the subject from the specific role of the clergyman as he seeks to function as pastor-counselor in the grief situation. Either not being trained in systematic observation or not having the technical psychological background necessary for the conceptualizing of the emotional reaction, the majority of pastoral writers fail to offer a precise definition of the response in such a way that overt behavior is linked with internal psychodynamics. Only a few of the materials attempt to present the topic in a manner useful to further psychological investigation.

Therefore, the purpose of this book is to undertake to attach as precise a meaning as possible to the word "grief," to link the overt and observable behavior with the inner dynamics, to connect the present experience with its antecedents, and to do so in such a way that further investigation may be expedited.

Finally, it will seek to relate an understanding of personality development and the role of language in this development not only to the arousal of grief but also to the needs of the bereaved person and to the manner in which these needs might be most adequately met. It is hoped that such a presentation would be useful to a number of persons: psychological investigators of emotion, psychotherapists, physicians, ministers, funeral directors, and all the others who in their professional roles or who because of personal relationships are called upon to deal with the grief-stricken.

Although a few books and articles that deal with grief are readily available to the interested person, some of the writings which make important contributions to an understanding of the reaction are more difficult to find. Some examination and evaluation of several representative approaches from various fields will provide a foundation for understanding the constructive portion of this book. Therefore a summary of selected writings is presented in chapter 2.

Chapter 3 is an elaboration of one concept of the development, nature, and dynamics of personality in terms which are felt to be particularly appropriate to an understanding of the reaction of bereavement. Building upon this theory of personality, the nature of grief as separation anxiety is proposed (chapter 4), followed by a discussion of guilt, or moral anxiety (chapter 5), and existential anxiety (chapter 6) as constituents of the grief-anxiety reaction.

The last chapter (7) outlines some of the implications of the concept of grief as anxiety for psychotherapists, ministers, and others who deal with persons in this situation of stress. The relation of talking to the several needs of the bereaved is discussed, and an approach to ways of preparing for grief is made.

It is hoped that this contribution to dialogue in this particular area of human distress will provide a theoretical formulation which may lead toward the increasing clarification and more adequate handling of these feelings which most of us have experienced and which we shall certainly experience again.

2
The Concept of Grief:
A Review of the Literature

It would certainly create a false impression to state that no one has been interested in the subject of grief or in grief-stricken persons. However, when one compares the amount of investigation and writing concerning this reaction with the great mass of material dealing with other human emotions and situations, it can readily be seen that grief has received relatively little attention. A selective review of some of the more important contributions from the fields of psychology, psychoanalysis, medicine, and pastoral care, however, do provide a background for understanding further elaborations.

PSYCHOLOGY

A psychological presentation of grief goes back to Charles Darwin, in 1872, as he related weeping and mental suffering, suggesting that fear is the form of suffering to which he was referring.[1] Alexander Bain, one of the early British psychologists, sought to express something of the source of grief in the loss of or separation from some object or person, with the sorrow being in proportion "to the power of the attachment."[2] That which we lose is our comfort and pleasure, which found its source in the other.

In the earliest article, and incidentally, one of the few in a psychological journal, Borgquist linked the subjective state of despair, the desire not to live, "the feeling of being helpless, hopeless, forsaken," with the total physiological response.[3] His observations led him to relate the death of a significant other with the subjective sense of one's own dying and the dread a person feels in the face of his inability to cope with the threatening situation. The need of the grief-stricken is for another person who can enter into this situation of crisis and protect him from the threat of his own extinction.

A rather extensive discussion of sorrow was presented by Alexander Shand in 1914, dealing with personality from a psychodynamic point of view. While using neither psychoanalytic nor contemporary psychological terminology, an inter-

---

[1] *The Expression of the Emotions in Man and Animals* (New York: Appleton, 1899), p. 146.

[2] *The Emotions and the Will* (London: Longmans, Green, & Co., 1875), p. 146.

[3] Alvin Borgquist, "Crying," *American Journal of Psychology*, XVII (1906), 163.

esting exploration of the conflicting inner impulses of sorrow was made. A primary human drive is that toward joy; its frustration is the source of sorrow.[4] This frustration in turn stimulates the attempt to maintain union with the lost person, since there is a tendency in all joy to restore its own state of being.[5] Although Shand saw fit to describe sorrow and fear as two distinct emotions, he did show a relationship between them. The nature of sorrow was stated in terms of a call for help. But then it was noted that one of the varieties of fear is also a cry for assistance.[6]

Leonard Troland has defined sorrow as "an affective state, resulting from the removal of an accustomed stimulus which strongly conditions one or more positive retroflex mechanisms."[7]

One develops a certain pattern of behavior built around successive and meaningful interaction with another person. This pattern is learned according to conditioning principles. When the other dies, the bereaved person's attention is forced upon the deceased by the series of events, thus serving as a constant stimulus to respond according to the previously conditioned pattern. In the actual absence of the other, however, these responses cannot be carried through. Therefore the result is that of frustrated impulses and of behavior which seeks to reduce the tension set up.

One of the distinguished early American psychologists was William McDougall. His reasoning seems to have been that sorrow is an inner condition comprised of both tender-emotion

---

[4] *The Foundations of Character* (London: Macmillan & Co., 1914), pp. 331-32.
[5] *Ibid.*, pp. 329, 334.
[6] *Ibid.*, p. 317.
[7] *The Fundamentals of Human Motivation* (New York: Van Nostrand, 1928), p. 448.

21

and negative self-feeling, forming such a unique subjective experience that the tendency has been to give it a name of its own. Although it is an affective condition, it is not a distinct and separate emotion, but simply a convenient term used to designate these combinations of other emotions cued off by a particular event. His perceptiveness in seeing the complexity of a person's emotional life is helpful, and he reflects an element of the concept of self-loss. For when there has been the loss of a loved one through death, "few can avoid some negative self-feeling under such conditions, for a part of the larger self has been torn away, and some thought of some effort which might have been made but was not is very apt to increase the intensity of this painful negative self-feeling." [8]

A name which stands out among the early investigators of grief from a social orientation is that of Thomas D. Eliot. As early as 1930, he published an appeal for an empirical study of grief, recommending a sociological appraisal of society's help to the bereaved.[9] He followed this in 1933 wtih a reference to the neglect of the reality of death in psychological literature, and called for as much investigation and open discussion of the mental hygiene of grief as there had been in regard to sex.[10] Unfortunately, not many professionals appeared on the scene to take up the challenge with which Eliot confronted them. Apparently there is good reason to believe that death and grief are more anxiety producing and, therefore, more to be avoided than the traditional "taboo topic" of sex. Eliot himself, however, continued his own investigations.

In an approach to a definition of grief, he states:

[8] *An Introduction to Social Psychology,* 22nd ed., enl. (London: Methuen, 1931), pp. 130-31.
[9] "The Adjustive Behavior of Bereaved Familes," *Social Forces,* VIII (1930), 546.
[10] "A Step Toward the Social Psychology of Bereavement," *Journal of Abnormal and Social Psychology,* XXVII (1933), 380.

Psychologically, bereavement is a major type in the general class of traumatic frustration-situations. Arrested impulse or thwarted habit is at the root of all sorrow. Bereavement is one's own blocked wish for response following death of the loved object. The loved one is gone, but the associated memories and habits and needs remain alive as a real complex in the mind of the bereaved.[11]

Even though the term "loved one" is used, it is recognized that within the interaction of two or more people the emotional pattern is not a simple one, nor all positive. "One must recognize that in thousands of 'normal' families, affection is mixed with indifference or with other less attractive sentiments which are ignored in our cultural stereotypes of family life." [12]

Hostility, guilt, relief are a part of the total situation. In the light of this, it seems strange that Eliot should say: "Intensity of sorrow tends to vary directly as intensity of prior love and joy." [13] He modifies the terminology somewhat when he indicates that where persons have become dependent upon one another, grief will be "intensified by the sense of emptiness, helplessness, or fear." [14] Dependence, however, is not identical with love, and although persons who love one another are usually dependent upon one another, the emotional involvement may also have strong elements of, indeed may even be dominated by, negative emotions.

Extreme self-centeredness is a predominant characteristic of the bereavement reaction. This is not said in a condemnatory way or to imply that the grief sufferer is normally a selfish person. It is simply a normal reaction under the circumstances, and "is understandable as a self-defense of the personality

[11] "Bereavement: Inevitable But Not Insurmountable," *Family, Marriage, and Parenthood,* ed. Howard Becker and Reuben Hill (Boston: Heath, 1948), p. 643.
[12] *Ibid.,* p. 661.
[13] *Ibid.,* p. 644.
[14] *Ibid.*

against a mortal attack on its inner integrity, a conflict within one's central citadel of values and of control." [15]

Another characteristic response of the person undergoing grief is the experience of the loss of meaning in much that previously had seemed important. There is the sense of "emptiness, deadness, futility." [16] This may even encompass one's own life, the loss of the sense of value of one's self, and the impression that one's life is not worth sustaining. [17]

The work of mourning is described by saying that "each unit of affectionate attachment to the deceased, upon being revived in memory and grief, is diffused and reattached, or at least loosened ready for transference to new objects." [18]

This cannot be the whole of the process, however, as Eliot seems to assume in other places. Not only must emotional ties be broken and the affection be reinvested, but repressed guilt and hostility must be brought into the open and worked out. [19] In addition, paradoxical though it may sound, while affectional ties are being broken, efforts to perpetuate the love-object in some fashion and the search for new objects of affection are taking place. [20]

Since grief is intensely self-centered and introvertive, any attachments or attractions to other persons, or almost any kind of group demands upon the bereaved . . . may serve a therapeutic purpose in detaching the fixations from the deceased and refreeing the energies of the bereaved from self-absorption." [21]

An important description and classification of the responses to bereavement resulted from an investigation made by David

[15] *Ibid.*, p. 652.
[16] *Ibid.*, p. 653.
[17] *Ibid.*, p. 654.
[18] *Ibid.*
[19] *Ibid.*, pp. 647, 655.
[20] *Ibid.*, pp. 649, 665.
[21] *Ibid.*, pp. 663-64.

24

Fulcomer. An analysis of observations, interviews, and material from daily journals of seventy-two subjects revealed four basic stages of adjustment to bereavement with several categories of adjustment identifiable at each stage.

The Immediate Stage, up to several hours following the death, included the Stoic, Dazed, Collapse, and Lacrimose responses. The Post-Immediate Stage, to the end of the funeral, included the Acquiescent, Excited, Protestive, Detached, and Despondent responses. Categories of Alternating, Enforced, and Attention-Getting described the behavior in the Transitional Stage, from the funeral to reentry into active life. The final stage was that of the Repatterning of behavior, categorized as Projective, Participative, Identification, Memory-Phantasy, and Repressive-Seclusive.[22]

Harold Orlansky points to anxiety as being the significant emotion as one confronts death, and he emphasizes the role of talking as a means of dealing with it. The prevalence of talking by the grief-stricken person is "the wish to relieve anxiety."[23] Hyperactivity arises from the same motivation, but talking seems to be an effective way of tension reduction because of its social meaning.

Silence . . . serves to separate the individual from society and makes his loneliness more complete. It is in this connection that the function of talk as a social bond and an affirmation of life, relieving the anxieties associated with silence and produced ultimately by the fear of death, becomes apparent.[24]

Henry Brewster points to the healing power of personal relationships to the bereaved. In order to accomplish this,

[22] "The Adjustive Behavior of Some Recently Bereaved Spouses: A Psycho-Sociological Study" (Ph.D. diss., Northwestern University, 1942), pp. 75-159. [Hereafter cited as Fulcomer, "The Adjustive Behavior."]
[23] "Reactions to the Death of President Roosevelt," *Journal of Social Psychology*, XXVI (1947), 254.
[24] *Ibid.*, p. 253.

dependency ties with the deceased must be broken, but it is not easily done when the dependency in the relationship has been excessive. In such cases there is a morbid reaction, a longer and deeper state of emotional preoccupation and a greater impairment of mental functioning.[25] By way of illustration he cites a case of pathological grief reaction in a girl. When her brother died, she sought to deal with the affect through the means of identification (development of shortness of breath and feeling of suffocation, reproducing symptoms of the brother's illness), repression (of her hostility toward him), and denial (of the reality of his death).[26]

In elaborating the interpersonal nature of grief, Volkart and Michael stress the social and cultural dimensions of the event as being particularly determinative of the psychological. Different patterns of family life produce variable emotional levels of self-involvement with other persons, and this is a major factor in the behavioral reactions of bereavement. For example, where a person grows up in a tribe where the life of the tribe is the highest value and where emotional ties are diffused among many persons rather than a few, the individual is less vulnerable to intense feeling of loss at the death of another individual. On the other hand, in our culture with the small family, small house, central role of the mother, much emotional investment in members of the family, maximal opportunity for the development of ambivalence through intense gratification and frustration in the family context, there is the breeding of overidentification and overdependency and the cultural definition of certain persons as irreplaceable. The death of a person then is a loss to the other members of the family, and is reinforced by the fact that it is defined by so-

[25] "Grief: A Disrupted Human Relationship," *Human Organization,* IX (1950), 19.
[26] *Ibid.,* pp. 20-21.

ciety as a loss. The need at the time of death is for the bereaved person both to replace the loss and to deal with his feelings of hostility and guilt.[27] With marriage and children, some of the primary attachments are dispersed through the lessening of interaction and normally of dependence, but new attachments and identifications are made, with their tendency to be of the same emotional order as the old.[28]

Complicating the behavioral responses to grief are the emotions surrounding role expectancy. The bereaved person has a social role to perform. So problems may arise not just because of the loss, "but by an awareness of one's inability to play the bereaved role properly." [29] Certain roles, of course, have been internalized by a person. But experiences in the relationship may have tended to contradict the role and emotions inappropriate to it developed. Because of social fear, many people sustain a relationship which does not seem on the surface to deviate too much from social expectation, but within which negative emotions must be repressed and guilt over the known failure to perform one's role adequately is increased. In bereavement, society says to feel the loss and express the sadness. But this is not always congruent with one's self-feelings, and our society has not provided for sanctioned channels of expression for hostility and guilt in the context of bereavement, at which time the accumulation of unexpressed emotion reaches its climax.[30]

Therefore it is not, as some earlier writers have indicated, that the intensity of grief is directly proportionate to the amount of love and joy which have existed in the relationship.

[27] Edmund H. Volkart and Stanley T. Michael, "Bereavement and Mental Health," *Explorations in Social Psychiatry*, ed. Alexander Leighton, *et al.* (New York: Basic Books, 1957), pp. 293-94.

[28] *Ibid.*, p. 295.

[29] *Ibid.*, p. 297.

[30] *Ibid.*, pp. 297-98.

Rather, a high initial vulnerability to the problems of bereavement is produced when the emotions of the bereaved person (sense of loss, hostility, guilt) are maximal and complex.[31] Problems are avoided and intensity of emotional reaction is reduced "when there is approximate congruence between the self and the social role of the bereaved." [32]

A number of early writers in the field of psychology recognized and sought to deal with grief. Tending to lack something of the precision of a well developed methodology and vocabulary, they nevertheless were keen observers and men of insight. Contemporary academic psychology, however, has almost entirely ignored the human reaction of grief. There are, of course, a few references to it in some of the books in the area of personal adjustment, but the statements are all too brief when one realizes the universality and the impact of the experience.

PSYCHOANALYSIS

The field of psychotherapy as a whole, and within it particularly psychoanalysis, has from time to time turned its attention to the dynamics of grief and mourning. Although for the most part it deals with abnormal expressions or the relationship of mourning to abnormal conditions, many insights are made available from this field. It would seem that these investigators could be logically grouped on the basis of how they have related grief and anxiety. There are those who understand some interaction between the two affective responses but who clearly distinguish them, those who identify the two, and those who make a contribution to an understanding of grief without direct reference to anxiety.

[31] *Ibid.*, p. 299.
[32] *Ibid.*, p. 302.

28

The Concept of Grief: A Review of the Literature

Grief and Anxiety Related but Not Identified

Any discussion of the psychoanalytic interpretation of grief properly begins with Sigmund Freud himself. To him, "mourning is regularly the reaction to the loss of a loved person, or to the loss of some abstraction which has taken the place of one." [33] Although he used the term "loved person," it should not be assumed that there is some pure relationship uncontaminated by other emotions. In spite of the fact that a person may be loved, there are usually elements of aggression and hate. This ambivalence, as we shall see, is normal within limits, but when the conflict is intense the mourning can become pathological. Mourning, although a drastic disruption of one's ordinary pattern of living, is such a universal response that it never occurs to us to consider it as being abnormal, since it also is usually a transient state dissipating itself over a period of time. [34]

Even though the reaction of grief is regarded as normal, it has as its distinguishing characteristics some of the same features as the pathological condition of melancholia: a painful frame of mind and the loss of interest in the outside world and one's usual activities. One's whole attention is given to one's response to the situation of the loss of the loved object. This is made necessary by the fact that the libido directed toward the lost object now has to be withdrawn and directed toward another object. [35] This arouses a natural resistance, since the lost object has in a way become a component of our own ego. [36] Thus, "the existence of the lost object is psychically prolonged," and it is necessary for all of the aspects of the

[33] *Standard Edition of the Complete Psychological Works,* XIV (New York: Macmillan, 1961), 243. [Hereafter cited as Freud, *Standard Edition.*]

[34] *Ibid.,* pp. 243-44.

[35] *Ibid.,* p. 244.

[36] *Ibid.,* p. 298.

object to which libido has been bound to become liberated.[37] This takes place bit by bit over a period of time; mourning is completed when this liberation of libido from the lost object has been accomplished and the ego is free again.[38]

Freud sought to distinguish between normal mourning and the pathological state of melancholia by pointing out that in the former one knows what he has lost, while the latter "is in some way related to an object-loss which is withdrawn from consciousness." [39] It is true that in mourning there is the external event of death, real loss, to point to, and that one *usually* is not able to see so readily the occasion for the reaction of melancholia. However, such an absolute distinction overlooks two factors. First, there certainly are pathological states of depression which are situational in nature as far as their onset is concerned, such as the neurotic depressive reaction and the psychotic depressive reaction.[40] To be sure, the external situation does not seem to contain within it factors which would ordinarily produce such intensity and duration of reaction, so it is assumed that significant and powerful unconscious elements are involved. But there is observable object loss. Coleman has clearly said that "most persons suffering from reactive depressions can describe the traumatic situation which led to their depression although they may not be able to explain their overreaction to the situation." [41]

The unconscious factors are usually those of repressed hostility toward loved ones and resulting feelings of guilt. The latter are dramatically intensified on an occasion such as the death of the person against whom the hostility is directed.[42]

[37] *Ibid.*, p. 245.
[38] *Ibid.*
[39] *Ibid.*
[40] James C. Coleman, *Abnormal Psychology and Modern Life,* 3rd ed. (Glenview, Ill.: Scott, Foresman, 1964), pp. 227, 229-30, 341.
[41] *Ibid.*, pp. 229-30.
[42] *Ibid.*, p. 229.

Second, Freud seems to be inconsistent when he says "there is *nothing* about the loss that is unconscious." [43] He has as much as indicated unconscious elements himself, for the external situation alone does not account for the reaction of mourning in which internal, unconscious processes are at work. He himself has noted the presence of ambivalence in mourning. It would seem that the differentiation would be simply a matter of the degree to which morbid unconscious processes are involved, and not whether they are or are not.

Another distinction which Freud made between mourning and melancholia was that in the former "the world . . . has become poor and empty; in melancholia it is the ego itself." [44] This leads to a lowering of self-regard in melancholia, which mourning lacks. Again it should be suggested that observation of a number of people experiencing the grief reaction would note the existence of lowered self-esteem, and that the emptiness in the external world is felt *because* there is an emptiness in the ego.

Certainly Freud is correct in describing the difference between mourning and melancholia, but it is primarily a difference of degree rather than kind. The very dynamics which he describes as being involved in the origin of the pathological state are also to be found in "normal" grief, only in less degree and in a person with a stronger ego. The transformation of the object-loss into ego-loss takes place in normal cases as well as morbid ones, for there has always been at least a certain amount of the identification on the part of the ego with the libidinal object, even though he discussed this only in regard to melancholia. [45]

He goes on to point out what should be taken to be the significant difference between the two reactions: the degree to

[43] Freud, *Standard Edition*, XIV, 245. (Italics mine.)
[44] *Ibid.*, p. 246.
[45] *Ibid.*, p. 249.

which the identification is narcissistic in nature, with the identification actually being a substitute for object-love.[46] It is this high degree of narcissism which is absent in normal grief; in this Freud was correct.[47] However, there is always some degree of identification and therefore a sense of ego-loss in the case of any loss of libidinal object.

Concerning the role of ambivalence, the "loss of a love-object is an excellent opportunity for the ambivalence in love-relationships to make itself effective and come into the open." [48] The observation is made that "in melancholia the relation to the object is no simple thing; it is complicated by ambivalence. . . . Therefore, the exciting causes of melancholia have a much wider range than those of mourning." [49]

Granted, but the point made here in addition is that in mourning the relation to the object is usually no simple matter either. Since some degree of ambivalence is present in all relationships, it should not be surprising that beyond minimal limits of hostility and yet short of extreme repressed hostility there should be a "pathological *cast* to the mourning," [50] but without the mourning itself being considered pathological or melancholia.

The resolution of the process of mourning comes about in the following manner:

Each single one of the memories and situations of expectancy which demonstrate the libido's attachment to the lost object is met by the verdict of reality that the object no longer exists; and the ego, confronted as it were with the question whether it shall share this fate, is persuaded by the sum of the narcissistic satisfactions

[46] *Ibid.*
[47] *Ibid.*, pp. 250, 258.
[48] *Ibid.*, pp. 250-51.
[49] *Ibid.*, p. 256.
[50] *Ibid.*, 251. (Italics mine.)

it derives from being alive to sever its attachment to the object that has been abolished.[51]

However Freud admitted his inability to explain why the detachment of the libido from its object should be so painful, why it is that the distinguishing conscious characteristic of mourning should be mental anguish.[52]

Later Freud discussed mourning from the point of view of its relation to anxiety, asking the question of when object-loss leads to one and when to the other. Reference is made back to the infant's reaction of anxiety and apparent psychic pain when separated from its mother. He has not reached the point of learning to differentiate "between temporary absence and permanent loss." [53] The reaction of anxiety is learned in this "loss of the perception of the object (which is equated with the loss of the object itself)." [54] So far this is not interpreted as loss of love. The infant is not yet capable of making that interpretation. Later, loss of love becomes linked with danger and thus a determinant of anxiety.

Karl Abraham elaborated in some detail the role of ambivalence and introjection in mourning. His point of departure was Freud's assumption that an ambivalent conflict was inherent in melancholia, and since the bereaved person seeks to introject the lost love-object, in order to try to maintain it, the unconscious hostility toward the object is experienced as hostility toward one's self.[55] Abraham carries this insight over into normal mourning, where "the person reacts to a real object-

[51] *Ibid.,* p. 255.
[52] *Ibid.,* pp. 245, 306.
[53] *Ibid.,* XX, 169.
[54] *Ibid.,* XX, 170.
[55] *Selected Papers of Karl Abraham* (New York: Basic Books, 1953), p. 419. [Hereafter cited as Abraham, *Selected Papers.*]

loss by effecting a temporary introjection of the loved person." [56]

This process calls the dead back to life by setting it up within one's own ego. Without the love-object, life has no more attraction, but establishing the lost object in one's ego serves the purpose of making life meaningful again.[57] The process of mourning produces the psychological result: "My loved object is not gone, for I now carry it within myself and can never lose it." [58] Abraham has gone beyond Freud when he declares that "introjection occurs in mourning in the healthy person . . . no less than in the melancholic. . . . Its main purpose is to preserve the person's relations to the dead object, or . . . to compensate for his loss." [59]

Abraham seems to be saying that the distinction between mourning and melancholia, grief and a neurotic depressive reaction, is primarily a matter of degree. In either instance, whatever the cause of the object-loss or threatened object-loss, the mechanism of introjection is triggered. To the degree that there is hostility toward the love-object, then hostility is directed inward toward the internalized object, this being experienced as depression. Where the relationship has not had deeply morbid elements, then it becomes possible, according to Abraham, for the feelings of affection easily to shove aside the hostile ones, and thus dispel the feelings of depression.[60] This is what takes place in normal grief.

Helene Deutsch has pointed out the extreme variation of reaction in the situation of bereavement. If grief is excessive or delayed, it is an indication not only that the amount of

[56] *Ibid.*, p. 435.
[57] *Ibid.*, p. 436.
[58] *Ibid.*, p. 437.
[59] *Ibid.*, p. 438.
[60] *Ibid.*, p. 442.

ambivalence overshadows the positive force of the ties, but also that guilt might be involved to a higher degree than expected.

Psychoanalytic observation of neurotic patients frequently reveals a state of severe anxiety *replacing* the *normal* process of mourning. This is interpreted as a regressive process and constitutes another variation of the normal course of mourning.[61]

This would follow, since the neurotic is already a person with a high level of anxiety. The loss of an emotionally significant person, being a reproduction of the original anxiety producing situation—separation from the mother—would simply increase his anxiety to a level where the neurotic mechanisms were no longer adequate and an acute attack of anxiety would result.

In seeking to explore those situations in which a person does not show the usual overt manifestations of grief at the time of bereavement, Deutsch validly demonstrates her assumption that the affect of "unmanifested grief will be found expressed to the full in one way or another." [62] This is true since *all* affect has a "striving for realization." [63] Therefore, for adequate functioning, "the process of mourning as reaction to the real loss of a loved person *must be carried to completion*." [64] If one fails to do so, the "flight from the suffering of grief is but a temporary gain, because . . . the necessity to mourn persists in the psychic apparatus." [65] There it will continue to seek expression, and, in fact, will find expression in sub-

[61] "Absence of Grief," *The Psychoanalytic Quarterly*, VI (1937), 13. (Italics mine.)
[62] *Ibid.*, p. 13.
[63] *Ibid.*, p. 20.
[64] *Ibid.*, p. 21.
[65] *Ibid.*, p. 22.

stitute forms, frequently in the form of "unmotivated depressions."[66]

A more recent attempt to clarify the grief reaction by reference to psychoanalytic concepts is that of Jack Spiro.

Each of the two instincts, sex and aggression, gives rise to intrapsychic conflicts, and these form the two sources of the response of grief when a loved one dies. The energy of the sexual instinct, which is first directed inward in the narcissistic phase of infancy, is normally redirected outward toward a loved object, originally the mother and later others. This energy of the id constantly seeks expression, and it is the function of the ego to direct the time and form of expression. Under normal circumstances the ego is capable of performing this function in accordance with the demands of external reality while allowing the id its gratification. However,

in bereavement, the libidinal energy of the Id which was directed towards the loved object is suddenly interrupted by death. But this great amount of energy continues to seek satisfaction although the object of this satisfaction no longer exists. The death of a loved object destroys the equilibrium that the Ego has tried to establish between the Id and itself. The Ego then finds it difficult and painful, if not impossible to cope with the libidinal energy that seeks discharge.[67]

The ego becomes overwhelmed; it feels weakened and helpless and in danger. The awareness of this danger is anxiety, and anxiety is aroused at the death of a loved object because the intense and large amount of sexual energy becomes more than the ego can handle. The first source of the grief response,

[66] *Ibid.*, p. 16.
[67] "A Time to Mourn: The Dynamics of Grief and Mourning in Judaism" (Ph.D. diss., Hebrew Union College, 1961), p. 37.

then, is in the sexual instinct and the resulting conflict between the ego and the id.

This second source of the grief response is in the instinct of aggression. Spiro states: "There is a natural interplay within the psyche between the sexual instinct and the aggressive instinct. It is innately human to feel ambivalence toward the same object." [68]

This interplay between the sexual and aggressive instincts begins to take place in the latter part of the oral stage, where "the child's experience with taking in food or expelling it becomes the prototype of all later perceptions of reality," and more especially in the anal stage where the retention and expulsion of the feces is the occasion for the child's learning to relate to love-objects in a similar contradictory manner.[69] "The child grows to dread his aggressive feelings because, to him, it is equivalent to the loss of love." [70] In order to protect himself against his own aggressive feelings toward loved objects, an internal authority, a restraint, comes into being. This is the super-ego, and it is obvious that it is in continuous conflict with the id. Because neither the id nor the super-ego distinguishes between wish and deed, when a loved object dies the super-ego conveys the message that one's aggressive impulses toward the dead person were the cause of the death. "This intensification of guilt can lead to a state of anxiety similar to that felt as a result of frustrated libidinal forces." [71]

However, Spiro denies that grief and anxiety are absolutely identical saying that anxiety is merely an "emotional condition closely related to severe grief." [72] And, "grief involves intense

[68] *Ibid.*, p. 39.
[69] *Ibid.*, p. 41.
[70] *Ibid.*, p. 44.
[71] *Ibid.*, p. 49.
[72] *Ibid.*, p. 16.

dread which is similar to the feeling of anxiety." [73] This similarity, however, he feels

is only temporary if the expression of grief is successful. . . . While the immediate reaction to a bereavement is to feel perhaps that the total self is threatened and even doomed—as in anxiety—the adjustments that should take place in the normal process of mourning assuage this feeling which is eventually dispelled.[74]

Anxiety is defined by Spiro as "a feeling of intense dread, a feeling that the total self is threatened. The painful state of anxiety is also a reaction of helplessness to a traumatic situation." [75]

This traumatic situation, he makes clear, is not the external event of the death *per se,* but the ego's perception of being weakened and overwhelmed and incapable of controlling the intrapsychic conflicts. Spiro concludes: "We are now able to see the similarities between the different aspects of the response (grief) and the states of anxiety itself." [76] And, "we see that the intense suffering of grief is a result of a traumatic situation just as anxiety is." [77]

Several questions remain. Is grief only an emotion *similar to* anxiety? If so, how are they to be distinguished? Or, is grief a term to apply to an aggregate of several emotions, of which anxiety is one? If so, what are the other emotions involved, and how do they add to our understanding of grief?

Grief and Anxiety Identified

Several writers take the position that grief or mourning and anxiety are identical experiences. One presentation of this

[73] *Ibid.,* p. 17.
[74] *Ibid.*
[75] *Ibid.,* p. 52.
[76] *Ibid.,* p. 54.
[77] *Ibid.,* p. 55.

view is that of Melanie Klein. Adult mourning is seen as the reproduction of a separation experience which is analogous to the separation experiences of the infant, which Klein actually calls infantile mourning.[78] The fear "of losing his loved objects" she calls the "depressive position," and this is always coupled with a longing, "pining," for the lost loved object.[79] The early losses and fears of loss, infantile mourning and the depressive position are bound up first with weaning, mourning for the breast and all that it means, "namely, love, goodness, and security." [80] Second, in the Oedipal situation there is the fear of the loss of both parents.[81]

At the same time the child is in the process of incorporating his parents; he "feels them to be live people inside his body." [82] The behavior of the parents toward the infant, incorporated as a living part of his own self, is determinative of the outcome of infantile mourning.

The increase of love and trust, and the diminishing of fears through happy experiences, help the baby step by step to overcome his depression and feeling of loss (mourning). They enable him to test his inner reality by means of outer reality. Through being loved and through the enjoyment and comfort he has in relation to people his confidence in his own as well as in other people's goodness becomes strengthened, his hope that his "good" objects and his own ego can be saved and preserved increases, at the same time as his ambivalence and acute fears of internal destruction diminish.

Unpleasant experiences and the lack of enjoyable ones, in the young child, especially lack of happy and close contact with loved

[78] "Mourning and Its Relation to Manic-Depressive States," *International Journal of Psychoanalysis*, XXI (1940), 126.
[79] *Ibid.*, p. 130.
[80] *Ibid.*, p. 126.
[81] *Ibid.*
[82] *Ibid.*, p. 127.

people, increase ambivalence, diminish trust and hope and confirm anxieties about inner annihilation.[83]

In normal adult mourning the death of a loved person, a separation, involves the reactivation of all earlier "mourning" (separation) experiences. All early losses and threats of losses take over, and they are now experienced as contemporary threats to the integrity and existence of one's ego.[84] Since the unconscious experience is that of the loss of one's good inner world and the increasing dominance of internal "bad" objects, the inner world is perceived as in the process of disruption.[85]

Therefore, not only does the ego seek to "reinstate the lost loved object" [86] itself, but it also begins to try to bring back to life the earlier internalized good objects, originally the parents, who have been a literal living part of his inner world. "These too are felt to have gone under, to be destroyed, whenever the loss of a loved person is experienced." [87] The awareness of mental displeasure, pain, which is a part of the work of mourning, is explained by Klein as being

partly due to the necessity, not only to rebuild the links to the external world and thus continuously to re-experience the loss, but at the same time and by means of this to rebuild with anguish the inner world, which is felt to be in danger of deteriorating and collapsing.[88]

Klein seems to be saying something quite different from Freud when it comes to the matter of grief work. Whereas Freud emphasized the necessity of withdrawing libido from

[83] *Ibid.*, p. 128.
[84] *Ibid.*, p. 136.
[85] *Ibid.*, p. 135.
[86] *Ibid.*
[87] *Ibid.*, p. 136.
[88] *Ibid.*

the lost object, Klein speaks of the preservation of the loved object. Actually the positions are complementary. No one would deny that the reality of the death of the person must be acknowledged, and that energies that were expended upon the person when alive must now be directed toward other objects, and that certain satisfactions which derived from the life of the other in relationship with one's self must now be obtained elsewhere. Nevertheless, certain of the most important personal benefits deriving from relationship with the now dead person need not be relinquished, and thus libido may be utilized in the reestablishment of inner relationship with the previously incorporated aspects of the dead person.

Thus, while grief is experienced to the full and despair at its height, the love for the object wells up and the mourner feels more strongly that life inside and outside will go on after all, and that the lost love object can be preserved within.[89]

Although the first response to the death of a loved one is the threat of the destruction of one's own inner life, one's own self, the ego which has incorporated numerous good objects is able to call upon these as resources of strength as one by one they are seen through reality testing to have life, and therefore, "every advance in the process of mourning results in a deepening in the individual's relationship to his inner objects, in the happiness of regaining them after they were felt to be lost."[90]

This is the process of the renewal of inner life in the face of the threat of its death, a regaining of the self which was threatened with destruction.

Just as the ego is stronger to face the crisis of separation by death because of the predominance of early happy experiences of love and comfort in relation to significant persons who

[89] *Ibid.*, p. 143.
[90] *Ibid.*, p. 144.

have been incorporated as good objects, so also is the adult mourner strengthened against the threat to his inner life by contemporary relationships with people whom he loves and trusts, who share his grief, and whose sympathy he is capable of accepting. If he has such relationships, "the restoration of the harmony of his inner world is promoted, his fears and distress are more quickly reduced." [91]

Mourning is successful when the individual succeeds in establishing once again the lost loved person as an active force in his own ego, as well as reestablishing all of the internal good objects which he felt he had lost, including the internalized parents.[92] In successful mourning, the early anxiety responses of infantile mourning must be taken into account as complicating factors, pitted against the internal good objects and reduced by their assurance of security so that the deeply buried love connected with the happy experiences with one's parents can come out and assist the process.[93]

John Bowlby begins with a statement of his thesis: "Separation anxiety, grief and mourning, and defense are phases of a single process." [94]

The nature of anxiety is built upon the concept of a system of inherited instinctual drives whose energies constantly seek an object of expression. When such an object is present, the mother for example, ties are formed. When the object is not present, the "mother figure is temporarily unavailable, separation anxiety and protest behavior follow." [95] Anxiety, then, is simply the experience of instinctual drive without a channel of direct expression. When the object continues to be unavail-

[91] *Ibid.*, p. 145.
[92] *Ibid.*
[93] *Ibid.*, pp. 146, 151.
[94] "Grief and Mourning in Early Infancy and Childhood," *The Psychoanalytic Study of the Child*, XV (1960), 9.
[95] *Ibid.*

able, the responses are those of grief and mourning, apparently a deeper form of anxiety. This situation of loss of the mother figure on the part of the child differs in terms of the responses made "in no material respect . . . from those observed in adults on loss of a loved object." [96]

The conclusion from these definitions is that grief and mourning are terms used to designate separation anxiety where the object is clearly lost, and that the depression felt and observed is a major form of response to this anxiety.

In regard to the prototype experience in infancy, Bowlby believes that the loss of the breast is exaggerated by most psychoanalytic writers and that the real trauma is the "loss of close contact with the mother" and her expressions of love. When the child is between the ages of six months and four years, this loss of contact gives rise to separation anxiety and grief and mourning of high intensity.[97] Although the small child does not know death, he does experience absence, and these are identical experiences. Bowlby refers to Deutsch who used the term grief for the mature ego but only separation anxiety for early childhood. However, "when records of the responses to loss of objects by adults and young children are placed side by side, . . . the essential similarity of the responses will be clearly recognized." [98]

The psychological responses can be grouped under five headings:

1. Thought and behavior still directed toward the lost object (a sense of continuing presence);
2. Hostility (toward the lost object, others, and self, the latter experienced as guilt and unworthiness);

[96] *Ibid.*, p. 10.
[97] *Ibid.*, p. 13.
[98] *Ibid.*, p. 16.

3. Appeals for help (often in the form of unreasonable demands, not knowing what he wants, irritability and ingratitude toward those who try to respond);

4. Despair, withdrawal, regression, disorganization (brought about by the reality of the loss), futility and emptiness and inertia, loss of organized patterns of activity, especially those of a social nature;

5. Reorganization of behavior directed toward a new object (a reconstructed relationship with the image of the lost object, plus the first phase of a new object relationship).[99]

Josephine Hilgard *et al* conceive of death as one of several separation traumas which the child experiences and the successful handling of each of these prior to bereavement produces a "separation tolerance," a "prepared antidote to separation anxiety." [100]

Other Psychoanalytic Insights Concerning Grief

A number of writers have pointed out elements of the dynamics of grief without raising directly the issue of the relationship between it and anxiety, although in a few places such a relationship seems to be implied. Important insights dealing with various forms of pathological responses are described. However, each one also elucidates some of the dynamics of normal grief. Creegan's case presentation shows that in any grief reaction there may be aspects of the behavior of the mourner which can be viewed as symbolic acts that seek to deal with the loss by recreating certain part elements

---

[99] *Ibid.*, pp. 17-20.
[100] Josephine R. Hilgard, Martha F. Newman, and Fern Fish, "Strength of Adult Ego Following Childhood Bereavement," *American Journal of Orthopsychiatry*, XXX (1960), 792.

of the relationship.[101] Bergler's discussion of the element of aggression leads to the conclusion that the duration of mourning is not in direct ratio to the amount of love in the relationship, as some writers have suggested. His assumption is that the less complex the interaction between love and aggression, the more directly each can be expressed. The less the distortion of each of these affects, the more meaningful is the relationship. Therefore, when it is broken in death, less time is needed for the grief work.[102] Rosner introduces the concept of "mourning before the fact," the anticipation of the loss of a valued object and seeking to protect against that loss by withdrawing libido from it and cathecting a substitute object.[103] Lehrman describes a reaction to untimely death, emphasizing the need for substitute objects to be immediately available.[104] Peck notes the morbid grief response when the person who dies had been identified with an original significant other, in the particular case he reports, the mother.[105]

MEDICINE

The classic study by Lindemann is now widely known and has been summarized in a number of books. In addition, it is available for thorough reading in two reprints.[106]

[101] Robert F. Creegan, "A Symbolic Action During Bereavement," *Journal of Abnormal and Social Psychology*, XXXVII (1942), 403-5.

[102] Edmund Bergler, "Psychopathology and Duration of Mourning in Neurotics," *Journal of Clinical Psychopathology*, IX (1948), 478-82.

[103] Albert A. Rosner, "Mourning Before the Fact," *Journal of the American Psychoanalytic Association*, X (1962), 569.

[104] Samuel R. Lehrman, "Reactions to an Untimely Death," *Psychiatric Quarterly*, XXX (1956), 568.

[105] Martin W. Peck, "Notes on Identification in a Case of Depression Reactive to the Death of a Loved Object," *The Psychoanalytic Quarterly*, VIII (1939), 2.

[106] Erich Lindemann, "Symptomatology and Management of Acute Grief," *Pastoral Psychology*, XIV (September, 1963), 8-18 [Hereafter

A provocative article by George Engel brings grief within the focus of medical concern. He uses the term "uncomplicated grief" where most others have said "normal grief." The reason for this is that grief can be thought of as normal in a statistical sense only, certainly not in relation to the total health of the individual. When considered in the light of this latter criterion, even uncomplicated grief is "a manifest and gross departure from the dynamic state considered representative of health and well-being." [107] The term pathological need not be shied away from, referring simply to the deviation away from the state of health of the organism. When grief is examined it is seen to fulfill "all the criteria of a discrete syndrome, with relatively predictable symptomatology and course." [108]

Engel feels that this view of grief has a number of implications for medical research and practice. Grief is a legitimate subject for such investigation. Its occurrence at the same time or immediately prior to other illness must be examined to the same degree as any other data. Since grief is so disturbing to a person's total adjustment, it could well be an etiological factor, and its physiological accompaniments may become the condition for more serious somatic changes. It is therefore firmly established as a physiological reaction, related to the operation of the central nervous system. Finally, since grief is a response to object loss, the medical team must see itself responsible for assuming the role of significant objects for the grief-stricken person if genuine healing is to take place.[109]

cited as Lindemann, "Symptomatology."]; and *Crisis Intervention: Selected Readings* ed. Howard J. Parad (New York: Family Service Assn., 1965), pp. 7-21.

[107] "Is Grief a Disease?" *Psychosomatic Medicine*, XXIII (1961), p. 20.

[108] *Ibid.*, p. 18.

[109] *Ibid.*, pp. 20-22.

PASTORAL CARE

One of the professional people most frequently in personal contact with bereaved persons is the minister. Among his major concerns has always been that of understanding the grief situation and seeking to be supportive to those involved in this form of emotional distress. It would seem logical to suppose that with this concern and involvement and with the increased tendency to relate psychological insights to the performance of the ministry, considerable material dealing with grief would be found in the literature of pastoral care. Although much of the writing deals with the funeral and the role of the minister as he functions to facilitate grief work, some important work has a clear bearing upon the nature and meaning of grief.

Wayne Oates is one of the few who places anxiety by name at the center of this affect: "The anxiety of grief is over a significant loss, or apprehensiveness over the threat of such a loss. The amount of anxiety determines any efforts to comfort the grief-stricken person." [110]

The anxiety of grief expresses itself in various ways as the grief process moves through six stages, each clearly identifiable even though they may not be entirely separated chronologically:

1. "The shocking blow of the loss in itself." [111] Oates feels that the anxiety has not been activated at this stage and that a person simply continues on automatically for a brief time.

2. "The numbing effect of the shock." [112] This stage is the organism's emotional anesthesia, the protection against the dire

[110] *Anxiety in Christian Experience* (Philadelphia: Westminster Press, 1955), p. 48.
[111] *Ibid.*, p. 52.
[112] *Ibid.*

threat to one's self, a common enough defense mechanism against anxiety.

3. "The struggle between fantasy and reality." [113] Unbelief and denial can no longer stand unchallenged in the face of the fact, but the self does not give up part of itself without a struggle and therefore seeks to hold on to that which it has needed emotionally through fantasy.

4. "The break-through of a flood of grief." [114] This is the open feeling and expression of anxiety, the cathartic action.

5. "Selective memory and stabbing pain." [115] Following the waves of severe overt grief expression, there is a lessening intensity of anxiety as one begins to pick up the normal routine of life, but there remain occasional memories which bring with them brief periods of sharp mental pain. During this time feelings of hostility and guilt seek both expression and assimilation in an integrated manner into one's present self.

6. "The acceptance of loss and the affirmation of life itself." [116] Oates speaks of the psychological "death, burial, and resurrection of . . . selfhood in the process of grief." [117] The individual who has felt the life of his selfhood threatened by the death of a significant person now overcomes the threat "by having taken the lost image of the loved one into his own concept of himself." [118]

William Rogers' important contributions to an understanding of grief are based upon the concept of the development of the self out of the interaction of the organism with the material

[113] *Ibid.*, p. 53.
[114] *Ibid.*
[115] *Ibid.*, p. 54.
[116] *Ibid.*
[117] *Ibid.*
[118] *Ibid.*, p. 55.

of its environment. Life is viewed as interactional, with the human organism building

into its emotional constellation not only parts of its own body, but the objects of its environment, including other people. People and objects become an extension of one's own personality. Feeling tone develops around these persons and objects according to their importance in the individual's attempt to meet his emotional needs.[119]

Whenever a person loses by any means the physical reality of one of these emotionally significant persons or objects, it produces the response of perceived threat to the self into which they had been incorporated; this threat is experienced as emotional pain, and this is what we refer to as grief. The most dramatic, the most final and irreversible loss, and therefore generally the most painful, results from the death of a person with whom one is emotionally identified.

The important point to remember, however, is that grief is *not* the result of what happens to the loved one. It is rather the result of what happens to the bereaved. Something of great importance to the individual, something that is a part of his psychic life, has been torn out, leaving a great pain, the emotion which we call grief.[120]

Paul Irion also states as a prerequisite for understanding grief the proposal that the meaning of individual life is defined in terms of the lives of significant other persons. Among the complex of feelings which comprise grief are those of sorrow, which Irion designates as a positive feeling, and the nega-

[119] "The Pastor's Work with Grief," *Pastoral Psychology,* XIV (September, 1963), 19-26.
[120] *Ibid.,* pp. 19-20.

tive feelings of hostility and guilt.[121] Grief, then, seems to be defined not as a single emotion but as a total ambivalent and painful emotional condition, only one facet of which is sorrow, an undefined positive emotion. This reaction to personal loss brings about not only a disruption of usual behavioral patterns, but also "a dislocation of certain elements of the role of the self." [122] Therefore, if there is lack of integration or if morbid elements are already present in the personality, grief may produce deviant behavior.[123]

The process of mourning involves learning to live with memories of the deceased and with the affect connected with them, both positive and negative. Until the memories are called to mind and reviewed and the emotions expressed, the images will continue in a self-disruptive manner. Reviewing and expressing is done most effectively when they are done verbally with another person, providing catharsis, insight, and a supportive relationship.[124]

Among the dynamic forces at work in the grief reaction, Irion lists fear. First is fear of death as such. The word "ontological" is used to clarify what is meant, a "fear which has its roots in the very nature of man's being as a finite creature." [125] Although various forms of expression of this fear may be culturally conditioned, the fear itself is not.[126] It is a universal, pervasive fear which cannot be removed.[127] We can only seek to evade it or understand it. Evasion, however, is made difficult by the reality of the death of someone very close

[121] *The Funeral and the Mourners* (Nashville: Abingdon Press, 1954), p. 31.
[122] *Ibid.*, p. 33.
[123] *Ibid.*
[124] *Ibid.*, pp. 36-37.
[125] *Ibid.*, p. 48.
[126] "In the Midst of Life . . . Death!" *Pastoral Psychology*, XIV (September, 1963), 8.
[127] *Ibid.*, p. 66.

to us, an event which tends to personalize death and stimulate the fear of our own.[128]

Another fear which is involved in grief is the fear of the dead person. This is largely unconscious in our sophisticated age, but it can be seen demonstrated where there are feelings of guilt and the bereaved appears to be attempting to placate the spirit of the dead through various acts of compensation.[129] It seems as if Irion might have sought to go further along this line of thought and put this concept on a firmer psychological base. Rather than leaving the matter sounding as if there is some dread of the dead passed on to us by our primitive ancestors, it would seem as if a case could be made for this fear being simply what he gave one clue as its being—guilt— fear of one's own conscience, a clearly interpersonal aspect of the self, into which the emotionally significant dead person has been introjected and where he lives on in a threatening way for the bereaved. It is actually a part of himself that he fears, the living incorporation of the now physically dead person, the part of himself with which the dead person has become identified.

The third form of fear which is found in grief is the most common according to Irion, although it is difficult to see how it could be more common than ontological anxiety. We fear our own suffering and loneliness.[130]

At this point Irion appears to contradict his earlier conclusion that grief is a term used to describe a complex of different emotions, for he says, "Let us turn our consideration now to feelings which are not integral parts of every instance of bereavement," [131] as if grief were actually the forms of fear

[128] *The Funeral and the Mourners,* p. 48.
[129] *Ibid.,* p. 49.
[130] *Ibid.*
[131] *Ibid.*

which he has been discussing, and as if these feelings which follow "are not integral parts of every instance of bereavement, but which are very frequently seen in mourners." [132] These feelings of ambivalence (love-hate), hostility, and guilt are not at all minimized. They are extremely complicating factors and can even be dangerous to the mourner, but the implication is that *they are not the grief itself.* Issue should be taken here only at the point of Irion's declaring that they are not universally found in bereavement. They may not be intense enough to cause complications in grief work, but it is difficult to see any close relationship without at least some ambivalence and guilt. Irion himself recognizes this later when he declares that "if we accept hostility in the broader sense, as a symbolic representation of the outgrowth of the frustrations which are found in all of life, we can accept the universality of the phenomenon." [133]

He then goes on to make the retraction of his earlier view about the lack of universality of ambivalence and guilt practically complete by saying, "feelings of hostility are almost inevitably complicated by feelings of guilt." [134] This is true because there are frustrations, disagreements, irritations in every intimate relationship. Normally, guilt is not experienced in most of these because there are always opportunities for reconciliation. But death brings these opportunities to an end, while the ambivalent feelings continue. Thus, without the chance for forgiveness, restitution, reconciliation, there is the growth of guilt.

Irion makes a provocative suggestion by relating various grief reactions to Horney's conceptualization of the predominant interpersonal behavioral patterns which people exhibit:

[132] *Ibid.*
[133] *Ibid.*, p. 52.
[134] *Ibid.*

moving toward, against, and away from people. In the normal person where each of these reactions is called upon in appropriate situations, we might see something of a mixture of these in the reaction to grief. But in those persons where one pattern of response to persons clearly is dominant, we should be able to predict the predominant pattern of the grief reaction: dependence and a bid for sympathy, hostility and irritability, or withdrawal and isolation.

Edgar Jackson has continued the task originally undertaken by Freud, that of delineating the grief reaction by seeking to differentiate grief from the emotional states that are similar to it. The first of these is anxiety. Grief has much of the same quality of threat to that which the individual perceives as being tied in with his own existence. However, he feels that grief differs in that "it is usually related to a specific fact of experience and therefore does not violate the reality sense." [135]

This distinction seems to overlook at this point, first, the unconscious factors which the external occasion of death arouse, and second, the fact that an eruption of an acute attack of anxiety may also occasionally be linked with "a specific fact of experience."

In regard to the first point, Jackson makes a distinction between normal and abnormal grief which seems to be based upon the assumption that there is a clearcut disjuncture between the two. He seems to be indicating that normal grief can be explained entirely by reference to the "objective" facts of the external situation and the conscious motives and emotions of the person who grieves, while abnormal grief is the expression of "unconscious fears related to unresolved early experience." [136] At this point Jackson is following Freud too closely and uncritically, for this is precisely the distinction

[135] *Understanding Grief* (Nashville: Abingdon Press, 1957), p. 19.
[136] *Ibid.*

which Freud made between mourning and melancholia and which has already been elaborated and criticized.[137]

It seems somewhat closer to human experience to place the concepts of "normal" and "abnormal" on a continuum, and admit that even a "normal" reaction has its unconscious elements and its references "to unresolved early experience," or at least to interpersonal experiences prior to the death which is the precipitating factor for the reaction. Even in "normal" grief there are elements of hostility and guilt that are not immediately conscious to the person grieving. Yet these remain within "normal" bounds because they are not so excessively intense that they are not amenable to "working through" by means of our usual relationships, institutions, rituals, and customs within a reasonable period of time.

In regard to the second point, we should remember that a key word in the definition of anxiety is *perceived*. That internal or external event which is *perceived* to be a threat to our being arouses the emotional pain which is the warning signal to danger to the self, or anxiety. The death of someone with whom we have been linked emotionally is not *necessarily* a greater objective threat to our being than any one of a number of possible events. Thus, to say that grief has reference to "reality," while overt anxiety which is aroused by other internal or external events does not, simply is not accurate. Although some persons may experience an acute attack of anxiety and not be able to point to a precipitating event, sometimes they can, even though they may not be capable of giving an adequate explanation of why such an external event should set off so intense a reaction.

So it may be with grief. A person is aware of his feelings and the precipitating factor. But still the particular intense

[137] See pp. 29-33.

individual response is not adequately explained. The external event of death does not *cause* tears, because some in grief do not cry. Death does not *cause* hyperactivity, because many in grief react by physical retardation. Death does not *cause* expressions of self-recrimination, because many do not respond in this way.

Even in normal expressions of grief unconscious factors are involved, and the particular responses of any given person are linked with earlier experiences which the person has learned to perceive as threats to his being and to which threats he has learned tendencies to respond in certain ways. Therefore, Jackson's conclusion that "normal grief and anxiety are clearly different as they relate to the reality factor" and it is only in abnormal grief that "the loss may serve as a precipitating factor that releases unconscious fears related to unresolved early experience" [138] must be rejected. He himself recognizes this since at a later point he shows that the experience of personal loss triggers hitherto repressed emotions, those that root as far back as the preverbal period.[139]

Jackson also seeks to distinguish between grief and depression. Grief and depression are clearly not identical, although there are similarities of response on some cases, with depression as such frequently involved at least to some degree as a part of the grief reaction. Jackson is probably correct, however, in indicating that the loss of self-esteem which is so characteristic of depression should not be linked with depressive elements of grief, although he seems to go too far in excluding this factor entirely.[140] Again he has followed Freud's distinction between mourning and melancholia without adequate criticism. The major point which is *not* made in this discussion is that anxiety

[138] *Understanding Grief*, p. 19.
[139] *Ibid.*, pp. 30-31.
[140] *Ibid.*, p. 20.

itself is the source of depression. Jackson has said this without saying it. "For as anxiety proceeds from a sense of danger to the value structure of the individual, so the state of depression grows from a feeling of injury or dislocation to the narcissistic or self-regarding element of the personality." [141] Such a clear distinction between these two intrapsychic sources as Jackson must feel that he is making is not obvious to this observer. Actually, any perceived threat by the individual to his psychic structure, or self, or style of life is experienced as anxiety. This perception of threat could hardly take place without involving that upon which he has placed value, for value *is* value because it is related to the sustaining of oneself as a person, which *is* the "self-regarding element of the personality." One direction in which anxiety may motivate the person is through attack, aggression, upon the source of the threat. But since that source is unconscious, the aggression is either displaced upon another object (the source of the hostility toward others in a number of the forms of the grief reaction) or upon one's self, the latter being experienced as depression (the source of depressive symptoms in much grief).

Jackson posits four dynamic factors which influence the grief reaction. The first of these is the personality structure of the bereaved, indicating that where a morbid interpersonal relationship has led to a weak ego there is danger of an abnormal grief reaction. Second, social factors of crisis, support, and expectation affect the nature and intensity of grief. Third, the role which the deceased has played in the life system of an individual, and fourth, the value structure of the individual affect the dynamics of grief.

In the attempt to understand grief it is necessary to include the time dimensions of both past and future. The past has

[141] *Ibid.*

already been referred to, and will be again and again. Since grief is primarily the response of the individual to severe deprivation, it is necessary to look to that person's early life experiences to discover how he has learned to deal with deprivation, the degree of tolerance or intolerance which has been established. Much of this pattern of response has been developed even before the child has learned to talk and is "assimilated from the actions and attitudes of adults in the family constellation." [142] Later patterns of behavior are based upon the degree of security and self-esteem the child has come to know in relationship with his parents. He learns to know who he is and something of his value as a person by the responses of his parents to him. Where these are loving and his needs are met consistently, security and self-esteem come into being. These are necessary for dealing effectively with mourning, whereas uncertainty and insecurity in relationships and a low sense of self-esteem resulting from lack of love and acceptance and inconsistent behavior on the part of parents make a person particularly "vulnerable to the strong emotions released by a major deprivation experience." [143]

Not unrelated to the past experiences which have produced a particular personality and its tolerance for deprivation, but having something of a future dimension to it is the fact that one's response to the death of an emotionally related person cannot be completely understood "without taking into account the attitude of the bereaved toward his own eventual death." [144] The dynamics of one's understanding of his own finite nature are always involved.

What Jackson seems to be referring to in these sections is anxiety, although he does not use the word. Security and

[142] *Ibid.*, p. 35.
[143] *Ibid.*, p. 37.
[144] *Ibid.*, p. 35.

insecurity in relationships is simply another way of speaking of the level of basic anxiety which is produced in the person through his early relationships and life experiences. One's attitude toward one's own death involves a greater or lesser amount of what is termed existential anxiety, the recognition of the reality of our own non-being. When he says that "affirmation, acceptance, and affection" [145] are the parental attitudes necessary for producing the types of personality which can do grief work effectively, it is another way of saying that these produce a person with a relatively low level of basic anxiety which is not raised to an unduly threatening level by loss. When the core of the grief feeling is described as a "feeling of acute pain," [146] this is precisely the way the subjective experience of anxiety is described. The *sine qua non* of grief is not depression, or feelings of hostility, or other emotions and overt behavior that may accompany it, but it is this "feeling of acute pain" accompanying the loss of an object of value to us, thus an object which is related to our own selfhood. The core of the grief experience is anxiety. The relation to our own selfhood of the lost object and that which is so threatening as to cause the psychic pain which is anxiety is clarified by Jackson's discussion of identification in which he refers to the personal experience of the death of a significant person: "In your death something in me also dies." [147] This is expressed in a different way by the statement, "bereavement is an amputation of a part of the emotional structure of life." [148] This is literally true to the degree that we have incorporated the responses of another toward us as a part of our own being. Thus the pain felt is "the pain of separation." [149]

[145] *Ibid.*, p. 40.
[146] *Ibid.*, p. 47.
[147] *Ibid.*, p. 60.
[148] *Ibid.*, p. 66.
[149] *Ibid.*

As the process of identification has brought us to the place as persons where this statement at the time of loss could be made, it stands to reason that one method of coping with the sense of personal deprivation is by further identification with the deceased. And that, of course, is just exactly what is observed in the behavior of bereaved persons. The purpose is to seek to restore in one's self "the significance of the lost object." [150]

Another method of combating the pain of grief is by substitution, relating the internalized ties to the significant other to some new external object.[151] Within limits this may facilitate grief work, but where the substitute becomes the center of one's total emotional investment, grief work is inhibited.

An interesting contribution which Jackson makes to the understanding and handling of grief is the role of values, meaning, purpose, faith in human life. Man can be understood as a being who seeks for meaning and coherence in life experiences. Without them life crumbles and the desire to live is weakened. This, in fact, is what frequently happens to a person when an emotionally significant person dies. A symptom of grief is the sense of the loss of meaning. If a person has no clearly thought out value structure which transcends immediate gratification, and if he has no real awareness of a meaning in life, then the loss by death of a significant other is the loss of all meaning, and grief is intensified. On the other hand, if one's value structure and sense of life's meaning encompass present relations with others but also go beyond these, a person has resources which temper the real loss and genuine pain, and the death of these persons is not seen as the end of all meaning.[152]

[150] *Ibid.*, p. 69.
[151] *Ibid.*, pp. 77-79.
[152] *Ibid.*, pp. 114-21.

SUMMARY

More than other observers, those within the field of pastoral care have linked the dying of an emotionally significant other with the subjective experience of the dying of part of one's own self, and have rather consistently pointed to this as the central feature of grief. Not only the perception of threat to the inner self, but also the obvious disruption of a life style coincident with the disappearance of an interactional field is anxiety producing. Although several writers in some manner discuss the subject of anxiety in relation to grief, only Oates speaks of "the anxiety of grief." Also linked to the external event are reawakened childhood fears, the remembered pain of helplessness.

Rogers stated the kernel of the theory which this book seeks to expand into a more complete theory, namely, that the development of the self evolves out of interaction with one's environment, including persons, and some of these others, depending upon their meaning to the individual, become extensions of one's own personality. The most significant aspects of one's environment become literally a part of one's personality and can be removed only with pain and damage to the emotional life.

Since grief is an interpersonal event, a threat to the self, it is an event that can be prepared for. The early experiences of love and trust and learned self-esteem and the development of a readiness to respond to others produce a person who is less threatened by a disrupted relationship. Warm relations with a number of people who meet different needs also furnish an inner strength with which to confront bereavement.

While investigators in all fields have mentioned the complicating and practically universal factor of guilt feelings, several in the area of pastoral care have been more sensitive to the fears concerning one's own death, which the death of a closely related person can stimulate. These fears perhaps are the source of the experience of loss of meaning which frequently accompanies bereavement. At this point is seen the constructive and therapeutic role of a value system and a concept of the meaning of life which transcends immediate gratification.

Thus are seen the three aspects of the anxiety which this book postulates as being involved in every grief response: separation threatening self-loss, guilt or moral anxiety, and fear of one's own death, existential or ontological anxiety.

Attention is focused on the fact that it is not the external event, what has *happened* to the deceased, which defines grief, but what is *happening* to the bereaved, the inner, psychic, or emotional events of the still living, but threatened person.

3

Anxiety and the Interpersonal Nature of the Self

Because the major thrust of this book is to elaborate in detail the concept of grief as anxiety, it is appropriate to attempt to make a coherent statement concerning the nature of anxiety itself. It is obvious that this cannot be done apart from a theory of personality which allows for a meaningful presentation of the development of anxiety. This theory must provide a conceptual framework and terminology which lends itself readily to psychological experimentation, which is compatible with human experience, and which is internally consistent as anxiety and grief are related.

It is not within the scope of this book to review even the several major approaches to a definition of anxiety. To do this would not only lead us far away from the central purpose, but it would be an exercise in redundancy, since this task has already been well accomplished by Rollo May in his classic work.[1] Rather, the task here is to select and describe a theory which can meet the criteria stated above.

Two clues are given to us concerning the concepts and terms of a heuristic theory. First, there has been the frequent reference in the literature dealing with grief to the centrality in the event of bereavement of the loss of or separation from an emotionally significant person. This has been true of academic psychology, psychiatry and psychoanalysis, and pastoral care. Second, a careful reading of Freud, undertaken originally because of his historical significance, because of the valid insights contained within his theories themselves, and because a number of other writers on the subject of grief have been so clearly dependent upon him, reveals a development of his ideas in a direction, which if followed, takes the reader beyond the literalistic, somatic basis of his theory into the realm of the interpersonal. Any number of his statements not only have these interpersonal implications, but actually seem to have more meaning when they are interpreted in these terms. Particularly does his explication of anxiety, when understood as an expression of disturbed personal relationships, the fear of separation, lend itself to a coherent description of grief as anxiety.

[1] *The Meaning of Anxiety* (New York: Ronald Press, 1950).

FREUD'S THEORIES OF ANXIETY

Summaries of Freud's first and second theories of anxiety have already been quite adequately detailed in other places.[2] It should be noted, though, that not only are there the two theories, but also a transitional stage. In the context of each of these chronological periods, it would be useful to look at and interpret a few representative statements demonstrating his observations which are of an interpersonal nature.

The First Theory (1894-1917)

A summary of the sequence of the mental events which produce anxiety is given in Freud's lectures at Clark University in 1909. A wish emerges, sexual in nature, which is in opposition to other desires of the personality. These wishes are perceived as threatening, so mental pain is experienced. The pain is avoided by the mechanism of repression, the pushing of the wish or conflict and its attached memories out of consciousness. Finally, the affect, the unattached mental energy, of the repressed idea is transformed directly into anxiety.[3] In this sequence it is clear that anxiety does not come into being until after repression has taken place and is nothing more than the apparently magically transformed affect of the repressed wish. There is a gap in the theory at this point, for Freud does not account for the process of transformation. He merely states that it takes place and leaves it at that.

His theory is that there is an accumulation of excitation, a raising of the level of tension, which is sexual and somatic in

[2] Seward Hiltner, "Some Theories of Anxiety: Psychiatric," and Ishak Ramzy, "Freud's Understanding of Anxiety," *Constructive Aspects of Anxiety,* ed. Seward Hiltner and Karl Menninger (Nashville: Abingdon Press, 1963), pp. 33-50, 15-29; May, *The Meaning of Anxiety, passim.*

[3] Freud, *Standard Edition,* XI, 24-37.

nature, and that this excitation is deflected from the psychic area, being employed in an abnormal manner, resulting in a decreased feeling of psychic sexual desire.[4] It is significant that he stresses "that the anxiety . . . can be traced to *no psychical origin.*" [5]

Freud has here laid the foundation for the somatic origin of all conflicts, for all disturbances to the self. That these physiological drives attached themselves to external objects and therefore had interpersonal repercussions, Freud made clear, but he was never able to explicate fully the meaning of interpersonal relations because of his somatic starting point. He undoubtedly did find disturbed sexual relationships in neurotic patients, but he chose to emphasize the etiological significance of unfulfilled, and therefore accumulated, excessive somatic sexual excitation, rather than the primacy of the disturbed interpersonal relationship, which would then naturally express itself in the inability of a person to make a full and adequate sexual adjustment.

As for anxiety,

The psyche finds itself in the *affect* of anxiety if it feels unable to deal by appropriate reaction with a task (a danger) *approaching from outside;* it finds itself in the *neurosis* of anxiety if it finds that it is unable to even out the (sexual) excitation originating from *within*—that is to say, it *behaves as though it were projecting that excitation outward.*[6]

In other words, the response of anxiety which is aroused by an internal situation with which the individual cannot cope is similar in quality to the response of fear to a specific external threat. Apart from the source of conflict's being in sexual ex-

[4] *Ibid.,* III, 107-108.
[5] *Ibid.,* p. 107.
[6] *Ibid.,* p. 112.

citation, the valid insight is that a determinative factor in the arousal of anxiety is one's perception of his own level of ability to cope with a stressful situation. One's self-evaluation is a factor. Freud's insight here is an important one, yet it is difficult to see how this self-evaluative factor fits in with the concept of anxiety which he was presenting at that time.

There are three factors of relevance to examine, however. The first is that this process which takes place in the present has a futuristic element. Very early Freud defined anxiety neurosis in terms of a syndrome whose nuclear psychic symptom is "anxious expectation" or "apprehension."[7] The person is looking for something painful to happen to him, an emphasis which was not fully developed and incorporated until the publication of his second theory twenty-two years later.

Second, this present pain which includes the element of expectation is also linked with the past. In his discussion of phobias, Freud explained that the emotional state is one of anxiety, and that

we often find the recollection of an anxiety attack; and what the patient actually fears is the occurrence of such an attack under the special conditions in which he believes he cannot escape it.[8]

As was indicated in regard to the concept of "anxious expectation," this reference to "recollection" points to a concept involved quite clearly in Freud's second and much later theory of anxiety. Here it does not seem compatible with the definition of anxiety as an automatic internal response to a high level of sexual excitation. Rather, despite the limits of this definition, he cannot help but allow incompatible insights to creep in. The two temporal dimensions to which he has

[7] *Ibid.*, pp. 92-93.
[8] *Ibid.*, p. 81.

referred could be united and the statement made that anxiety is the anticipation of or apprehension concerning the possible repetition of an unpleasant or painful emotion, an earlier form of which has already been experienced.

One method of presenting the manner in which the present affect of anxiety is linked with the past is by reference to its relationship to birth. At the core of the anxiety response is the repetition of an earlier, significant, and universal experience, "the precipitate of a reminiscence." [9] This earlier experience is birth, for it is in that event

that there comes about the combination of unpleasurable feelings, impulses of discharge and bodily sensations which has become the prototype of the effects of a mortal danger and has ever since been repeated by us as the state of anxiety.[10]

There is a deep insight in this reference to the past-dimension, as if one was being threatened at the very core of his existence.

Freud makes another statement which is difficult to understand in relation to his first theory of anxiety. Yet it contains the very heart of the meaning of anxiety as the fear of separaion from or loss of the significant other, and fits beautifully as a symbol into the conceptuality provided by the interpersonal context of the development of the self, and thus its basic interpersonal nature. "We shall also recognize it as highly relevant that this first state of anxiety arose out of separation from the mother." [11]

This last statement leads naturally into a discussion of the third factor to note in this first theory. There is an interweav-

[9] *Ibid.*, XVI, 396.
[10] *Ibid.*
[11] *Ibid.*, p. 397.

ing into his intrapsychic approach of references which are clearly interpersonal in nature. A most revealing passage seems to point clearly to the interpersonal nature of anxiety, but Freud, by virtue of his commitment to the somatic origin of the excitation, is not free to develop it fully. "Children themselves behave from an early age as though their dependence on the people looking after them were in the nature of sexual love." [12] The point here is not to take up the battle against sexual overtones in the relationships which children have, but it is to place the central emphasis on the relationship as such as being of primary importance to the individuals involved. Therefore, that which is most highly motivating is the goal of nourishing and sustaining the relationship through which the self of the child is being created and maintained, not the mere reduction of the posited increase in somatic, sexual tension. The important fact in the quoted statement above is "their dependence on the people looking after them." This is the insight that is logically linked with the very next sentence in the passage: "Anxiety in children is originally nothing other than an expression of the fact that they are feeling the loss of the person they love." [13] The anxiety is the fear that they are losing, are separated from, the person upon whom they have learned to be dependent for their own existence as persons. "They are afraid in the dark because in the dark they cannot see the person they love; and their fear is soothed if they can take hold of that person's hand in the dark." [14] For the child the proof of the security of the relationship upon which he is dependent must be more tangible than simply an inner conviction. No matter how reliable and consistent the parents have been in meeting his needs, so long as

[12] *Ibid.*, VII, 224.
[13] *Ibid.*
[14] *Ibid.*, p. 224.

he is really dependent upon them for sustenance, protection, and comfort, as well as his emotional needs, concrete expressions of the relationship remain an absolute necessity, and for the child there is no substitute for this. Indeed, even for the mature person, an inner conviction of the security of a relationship of love without the physical presence of the other and specific expressions of love has its limits, although these limits may have a great elasticity about them.

The child has not yet learned that dependability on the part of the other tends to guarantee dependability for the future. He has not yet learned to substitute the thought, the image, of the other for the actual presence of the needed one. Seeing the other, hearing the other, feeling the body of the other, is the only assurance of the reality of the significant person. Darkness, which blots out sight, is the equivalent of the loss of, separation from, the person who is needed.

Freud illustrated this point with the story of a three-year-old boy whom he heard calling out of a dark room: "Auntie, speak to me! I'm frightened because it's so dark." The aunt answered: "What good would that do? You can't see me." He replied: "That doesn't matter. If someone speaks, it gets light." [15] Freud interpreted the story: "Thus what he was afraid of was not the dark but the absence of someone he loved; and he could feel sure of being soothed as soon as he had evidence of that person's presence." [16]

It is separation from the emotionally significant person, separation in and of itself, that forms the threat to the self and which is experienced as anxiety, not merely the experience of an accumulation of ungratified sexual drive, because the existence of the self is dependent upon the existence of the relationship with the other. To say, as Freud does, that there

[15] *Ibid.*
[16] *Ibid.*

is excessive sexual instinct (libido) created by separation and the child turns "his libido into anxiety when he cannot satisfy it" [17] leaves too many questions unanswered. Why is excess libido turned into anxiety? What is the threat? If the answer be "disintegration of the ego in the face of overwhelming libidinal drive," precisely how has the ego come to have such a characteristic of perceiving strong drive as threat to its existence? How is repressed libido transformed from sexual desire into the experience of fear?

Let us clearly understand at this point, it is not basically an interpersonal situation that Freud has been describing as the *cause* of anxiety, but the condition of physical separation is merely the *occasion* when libido accumulates, and this internal energy is "transformed into anxiety," [18] or "it would be better to say discharge(d) in the form of anxiety." [19] Shifting Freud's emphasis, it could be stated that the real threat to a person *is* the loss of the sustaining presence, physically, and to an even greater degree, emotionally, of a person perceived as necessary to one's own existence, and undischarged libido merely being the stimulus to that painful memory, or the making present of the past threat.

The Transition Period (1917-1926)

Following the publication in 1917 of Freud's lectures delivered at the University of Vienna during the preceding two years where his first theory of anxiety was presented in its most complete form, we move into a period of transition prior to the statement of the second theory. This is not to imply that Freud's position had been static up until now. New elements

[17] *Ibid.*
[18] *Ibid.*, XVI, 409.
[19] *Ibid.*, p. 410.

continued to find their way into his statement of anxiety, a number of these difficult to resolve with his earlier assumptions and actually foreshadowing his second theory. However, in this period from 1917 until 1926, Freud published a formulation of his changing concepts of personality, providing him with the conceptual framework for the statement of a different theory of the nature of anxiety, one which is not only more open to an interpersonal interpretation, but at times seems to ask for it. In spite of this, however, Freud never completely broke with his grounding of personality dynamics, motivation, in somatic processes, of which the instincts were mental representations.

The major contribution to a new understanding of personality dynamics and thus of anxiety was the presentation in 1923 of a new set of mental constructs: id, ego, and super-ego. His concept of anxiety was modified and the following order of progression was given: the ego perceives danger; anxiety is the expression of recoil from it; the pleasure-pain principle calls the ego into operation to repress that which it perceives to be the source of danger. This order is clearly different from his previously stated theory in that repression now follows anxiety rather than preceding it. Therefore, anxiety can no longer be conceived of as being the transformation of repressed libido.[20]

The precise dangers are not yet specified, but a key idea expressed is that the ego fears being annihilated. Earlier it has been made clear that the occasion is separation from the mother and other significant persons. But why should this separation be so feared? Simply because somatically originated libidinal tension accumulates? This does not seem to be a meaningful account. Is not the heart of the matter the fact that the ego understands its own existence as dependent upon union with

[20] *Ibid.*, XIX, 56-57.

emotionally significant other persons, that having come into being in an interpersonal matrix, interaction with others, it cannot survive apart from relationships with others? In the infant and very young child, this relationship is real only with the assured physical presence of the other, and only gradually does he come to learn that separation, physical absence, does not necessarily mean the destruction of the needed relationship. Yet even when this lesson is learned, there remains the residue of the first interpersonal situation in which presence equaled relationship and thus the security of one's own existence. From time to time in life, in disrupted meaningful relations, the old fear is intensely aroused and one's own self is seen as being in danger of being annihilated.

The Second Theory (1926-1939)

The ideas which Freud stated rather briefly in this last work in 1924 were elaborated systematically and completely two years later.

Anxiety is "a special state of unpleasure with acts of discharge along particular paths." [21] It is *something felt*. It is nothing more nor less than a signal given by the ego in a situation of danger (or one interpreted as a danger) for the purpose of influencing the pleasure-pain mechanism.

A question of major significance is, of course, related to the original source of anxiety in each human life. Freud explained this by reference to the past-dimension in the life of every person. Affective states become a part of the psychic life of every individual very early in his existence as a result of those situations which allow an increase in tension to develop. Thus, anxiety is not created anew with each specific danger situation, making it necessary for the person to learn of the

[21] *Ibid.*, XX, 133.

danger right within the given situation itself. Rather, anxiety is reproduced as this earlier memory of danger is stimulated, not in the sense that the individual is able to remember the original event, but in the sense that the similarity of the present situation triggers the affect that was a part of the original configuration. With regard to anxiety the origin of the memory picture which carries this affect is the act of birth. The central feature of that event is separation from the mother and the flood of intense stimuli with which the infant alone is incapable of coping, a condition which is perceived as overwhelming, threatening annihilation. In other words, the origin of anxiety is in the pain of an original dangerous situation "and it is reproduced whenever a state of that kind recurs." [22]

The interpersonal origin of childhood fears is clearly stated:

They occur . . . when a child is alone, or in the dark, or when it finds itself with an unknown person instead of the one to whom it is used—such as its mother. These three instances can be reduced to a single condition—namely, that of missing someone who is loved and longed for.[23]

This is the key to the understanding of anxiety, according to Freud. He did, then, go on to relate the concept of separation to a physiological condition, which, of course, is always involved in the increased tension which is experienced painfully as anxiety.

The interpersonal implications of Freud's insights might be elaborated in the following manner. The infant's learning has been based upon the perception that he is totally dependent upon the mothering one, not only literally in a physical way,

[22] *Ibid.*, p. 134.
[23] *Ibid.*

but also for the very existence of the self as a psychological reality. A prime motivation for the individual is to maintain and enhance the unity, integrity, and efficient functioning of this self which is interpersonal in nature. Any threat to the relationship calls up the response which was the infant's first reactions to the absence of the mother—fear and panic. The external loss is perceived as threatening because it is understood as meaning self-loss, the breakdown of the self, because the person has learned as an infant the response of helplessness to separation from the mothering one. But the maintenance of the self, the individual must learn, is not made impossible by separation. He must move beyond the helplessness he originally learned in the face of the absence of the mothering one to the realization that the significant aspects of the other have now been introjected. The other is living as a part of the self, and even absence, broken relationship, death, while painful and involving an element of emotional impoverishment until other relationships are established, do not mean the death of the self which has been related to the other.

In Freud's analysis of anxiety, only one other relationship needs to be pointed out, that with regard to expectation. The dimension of the past (early experience, learning) has been described by reference to the event of birth and the Oedipal situation. Now it remains to show that it is not just remembering something in the past that is so painful. Anxiety is the fear that something will happen in the future. "The signal (of anxiety) announced: 'I am expecting a situation of helplessness to set in.'" [24]

Anxiety is both the remembering of the past painful situation and the anticipation that the pain will be repeated. The purpose of the arousal of the anticipated pain is, of course,

[24] *Ibid.*, p. 145.

so that the greatest pain itself, loss of the other, annihilation of the self, might be avoided by adjustive patterns of behavior.

A Critical Evaluation

Freud frankly staked the validity of his whole theory upon the organic, somatic origin of all increases of tension which provide the energy for human behavior. His first theory of anxiety reflected this principle clearly; somatic, sexual excitation is frustrated in its expression, its ideational content is unacceptable and is therefore repressed, but since energy cannot be destroyed, the affect became transformed and was physiologically discharged as anxiety.

However, Freud was so keen an observer that he began to note other factors which were related to anxiety: the relationship of anxiety to a situation of internal danger comparable to external danger; the reference back to the past learning experience, of which birth was the prototype; the reference to the future as the element of expectation in anxiety; the centrality of the concept of separation from the mother; the sense of helplessness which is involved. It was with great difficulty that Freud labored to get these concepts into harmonious relationship with his first theory. Of course, it is to his credit that he had the openness to allow these and other observations to lead him to a reformulation which was drastically different. By so doing he was freed to portray more clearly the interpersonal features of the situation. However, still being committed to the somatic origin of all motivation, rooted in instinct, he remained bound to the necessity of giving priority to the arousal of libidinal wishes as the source of the situation in which the signal of anxiety is given. Yet again and again it seems as if he is also saying that the loss of the libidinal object, separation from the mother and later from other emotionally significant persons, is the situation which the ego perceives as the danger to itself, the threat of self-annihilation through the loss of the other, and that the concepts of birth trauma and castration fear are powerful, dramatic, and dynamic symbols of the central meaning of *all* anxiety—fear of the loss of the significant other without whom the self cannot exist.

May has already raised the question as to whether Freud was not using both birth and castration as "symbolic for the separation from the loved object." [25] Although Freud may not consciously have come to the place where he could say that these were symbols, and only symbols, his increasing insight concerning the centrality of separation from an emotionally significant person continued to push him in that direction. May feels that this was a positive trend, allowing for the emphasis upon the infant's early relations with its mother as being of the utmost significance in the development of anxiety patterns.[26]

This stress on the interpersonal nature of anxiety, with the loss of the other being perceived by the organism as the equivalent of self-loss, intrapersonal disintegration, would not deny the validity of a description of the raising of the tension level of a physiological nature within the organism, an accumulation of undirected drive.

However, to call this somatic energy instinct is not helpful to a contemporary understanding of the immediate situation, and to say that it is this increase in drive which leads to the ego's perception of a danger is not compatible with the original infantile learning of the fear of separation. It is not the infant's increased physiological need which causes the mother to leave. When she is present, need arises and she meets it. So even

[25] *The Meaning of Anxiety*, p. 120.
[26] *Ibid.*, pp. 122-23.

though increased need is unpleasant, the presence of the mother assures its fulfillment. It is only when she is absent that need arises to high intensity because of her inability to observe its increase. Thus, the infant learns to fear her absence, for it is only at that time that need reaches highly unpleasant intensity. The separation leads to the fear of unfulfilled need, not *vice versa*.

Allport has pointed to "the essential emptiness of all instinct formulae." [27] To posit a universal instinct of sex or aggression, love or hate, does not say anything meaningful about a specific person in a specific situation at this very moment. "The really important questions concerning love—and concerning hate—are postinstinctive questions." [28] It is the contemporary expression, its form and motivation, which forms the significant material for investigation. This is not to deny a past learning, but the past learning has taken place in the matrix of a family where it is unavoidable that attachments, with both positive and negative elements, be formed. They are formed concretely as a function of the particular constellation of relationships in which the infant and young child finds himself. To say that these relationships are merely the result of an instinct seeking an object "is simply not helpful." [29] It is the interpersonal situation into which the child is born and his learning of relationship (his learning of dependence both physically and emotionally, his learning of the sense of helplessness in the face of separation from the ones upon whom he is dependent, his learning that the existence, the functioning, and fulfillment of his own self is only in relation to another) that are determinative of the nature of

[27] Gordon Allport, *Personality and Social Encounter* (Boston: Beacon Press, 1960), p. 207.
[28] *Ibid.*
[29] *Ibid.*, p. 208.

anxiety as separation fear and the situations which are perceived as threatening self-loss through the loss of the significant other. And, of course, it has been observed that Freud himself moved away from the primary emphasis on the role of the instincts in anxiety and toward the threat of separation, the perception of the loss of another, the disruption of an interpersonal relationship, as being a danger to the self, and thus, the significant factor in the arousal of anxiety.

THE INTERPERSONAL NATURE OF THE SELF

The preceding critical evaluation of Freud's developing concepts of anxiety is not to deny the physiological foundation for the development and functioning of human behavior, but it is to raise the issue of the learning in an interpersonal context of behavior tendencies which we term personality. The importance of relation with another as a factor in the anxiety reaction was not overlooked by Freud, but it has been pointed out that his own presuppositions limited the development of these interpersonal aspects.

Others not limited in this manner have gone further in the elaboration of a self theory that is built upon observations of interpersonal behavior, furnishing a meaningful conceptual framework out of which to understand the dynamics of anxiety, and, in turn, to understand grief as anxiety.

By the term "self" is meant the result of the individual person's differentiating not only his physical body, but also his own unique patterning of his perceptions and values centered about his lifelong task of creating, sustaining, and actualizing himself. It is the "I" which I think of when I am aware of myself, or which, even without conscious awareness, has learned to function as a whole system according to certain

78

patterns of self-consistency in order to maintain the integrity and unity of the whole organism.[30] This concept contains within it both of the uses of the word "self" in psychology: (1) self-as-object, when I think of "me," and (2) self-as-process, the learned pattern of functioning of the organism as it seeks to enhance itself according to certain learned values.[31]

A central factor to keep in mind is that the human infant is not born a complete self. He becomes a self by virtue of two factors, both of which are necessary: (1) physiological potential, a major element of which is the capacity for symbolizing behavior, of which language is a form primary in importance; and (2) the fact that the infant is born into a social community, a group of persons, a family, a neighborhood, and various social institutions, and with whom he will be forced to establish communication.

THE DEVELOPMENT OF THE INTERPERSONAL SELF

The individual human being is conceived of as being interpersonal in nature not only because he is capable of interacting and needs to interact with others outside himself, but primarily in the sense that his own individuality is constituted by other selves: ". . . the Self exists only in dynamic relation with the other. . . . [It] is constituted by its relation to the other; . . . it has its being in its relationship; and . . . this relationship is necessarily personal." [32]

[30] Prescott Lecky, *Self-Consistency* (New York: Island Press, 1945), p. 82.
[31] Calvin S. Hall and Gardner Lindzey, *Theories of Personality* (New York: Wiley, 1957), p. 468.
[32] John Macmurray, *Persons in Relation* (New York: Harper, 1961), p. 17.

This is made inescapable by the newborn's dependence for his very survival upon others and the combined necessity of and capacity for communication. Thus, a master key to understanding the development and functioning of the interpersonal, but differentiated, self is the dynamic character of language.

Differentiation of the Organism from the Environment

The infant's first responses are global ones, both toward himself and his environment without any distinction between what is inside the skin and what is outside. The first step toward selfhood is to learn to react to himself as a physical object, to differentiate the various parts of the body, and thus to distinguish himself from the surrounding environment. Especially significant in this process is the coordination of hand and mouth interaction. This interaction, well developed by six months, provides the basic material for "the differentiation of the infant's body from everything else in the universe." [33] There arises out of this coordination the delineation of two forms of experience: the self-sentient (of which sucking the thumb is the prototype) and the non-self-sentient. The former becomes the "pre-information or information which will presently be organized as the conception of the body," while the latter, the touching of something with the hand and the sucking with the mouth that which does not also feel touched and sucked, has reference to external reality.[34] Self-sentient activities will soon unite and become a significant key in the unification of all experience which is

[33] Harry Stack Sullivan, *The Interpersonal Theory of Psychiatry* (New York: W. W. Norton, 1953), p. 136. [Hereafter cited as Sullivan, *The Interpersonal Theory*.]
[34] *Ibid.*, p. 141.

understood subjectively as being mine and which is symbolized by the personal pronouns "my" and "mine." [35]

The self is not at first "inside"; as the child first learns to know it, it is the body. In time, however, . . . the ego is referred "inward." As language and the system of images develop, the child builds up an "inner world" in contrast to the "outer world." [36]

The Dynamic Role of Language

The development of language greatly facilitates this process because it enables the child to distinguish more clearly between "I" and "it" and "I" and "you," between word and meaning, to think of himself as differentiated, to express himself. Language makes it all more precise and more complex.[37] Illustrative of the inner thought processes at work is the way in which many children use their own names to refer to themselves before they use the personal pronouns "I" and "me." When these pronouns emerge, a giant step forward is taken by the child in forming and assimilating attitudes about and toward himself.[38]

It can be seen from the language being used in this description that taking place at the same time the child is learning to react to himself as a physical object, but then continuing for a lifetime, he is also learning to react to himself as a social object, a self, a person. He evaluates himself by the responses others make to him and the status they give to him. This is quite obvious. Since there is no self to begin with, no innate, developed attitudes directed toward the individual organism,

[35] *Ibid.*, p. 139.
[36] Gardner Murphy, *Personality* (New York: Harper, 1947), p. 586.
[37] Muzafer Sherif and Hadley Cantril, *The Psychology of Ego-Involvements* (New York: Wiley, 1947), p. 165.
[38] *Ibid.*, p. 177.

no conclusion can be drawn except that the material for the self-concept is given by the environment, the most significant part of which for the infant is the mothering one. "What happens to the infant is, to all intents and purposes, identical, whether the mother or the mother's helper is involved." [39] Therefore, she, and any other person who helps in the performance of the mothering role, is the source of the behavior toward the infant which the infant incorporates as his own responses to himself. John Macmurray is correct when he points out that "genetically the first correlate of the Self is the mother." [40] But it is also true that she is the first correlate of the interpersonal self. "Mothers are the persons who interpret us to ourselves. In so doing, they help us become the selves we are." [41]

Harry Stack Sullivan describes the formation of the foundation of attitudes toward the self in terms of the infant's responses to three aspects of the interpersonal situation with the mother: rewards, a gradient of anxiety, and intense, overwhelming, sudden anxiety. Out of these forms of perceived mothering behavior "there comes an initial personification of three phases of what presently will be *me,* that which is invariably connected with the sentience of *my* body." [42] The "me" is experienced, respectively in response to these three forms of the interpersonal situation, as "good-me, bad-me, and not-me." [43] They all come into being to varying degrees, dependent upon the quality of the interpersonal relationship between the mothering one and the infant; but they are linked

[39] Sullivan, *The Interpersonal Theory,* p. 120.
[40] *Persons in Relation,* p. 80.
[41] Earl Loomis, *The Self in Pilgrimage* (New York: Harper, 1960), p. 41.
[42] *The Interpersonal Theory,* p. 161.
[43] *Ibid.*

together as referring to the same person by "their relatedness to the growing conception of 'my body.'" [44] We see here the material out of which all experiences referring to the self are built, and the material is composed of the perceived behavior, the attitudes and acts, of the mother toward the child. The foundation of the self is comprised of the internalized responses of the significant other. The individual self is interpersonal at its core, arising out of and continuing to be dependent upon the other.

George H. Mead states that

self-consciousness is an awakening in ourselves of the group of attitudes which we are arousing in others. . . . The individual possesses a self only in relationship to the group of selves of the other members of his social group. [45]

Speech obviously increases the effectiveness of these self-reactions, which are responses to the reactions of significant others to the child. He quickly learns to use the same words about himself that others use in referring to him. At first, the self-directed words lack much of the intended meaning of the significant other who originally used them, but gradually the self-attitudes expressed by the words will tend naturally to be the attitudes adopted by the child rather than others. [46]

Once a child has begun to speak, his own speech becomes reinforcing for the attitudes that he expresses toward and about himself and for the behavior which is implied in his speech.

---

[44] *Ibid.*

[45] "Language and the Development of the Self" *Readings in Social Behavior,* ed. T. M. Newcomb and E. L. Hartley (New York: Holt, 1947), p. 189.

[46] Norman Cameron, *The Psychology of Behavior Disorders* (Boston: Houghton Mifflin, 1947), pp. 98-100.

The individual hears his own sounds just as well as he hears the sounds of others, and they are no less a stimulus to him when used by him than when they are expressed by others. When we hear a word, whether someone else speaks it or whether we ourselves speak it, we hear it in reference to ourselves. Just as there is set up a tendency to respond to another's speech, so also is there set up a tendency to respond to our own.[47] Our language becomes a means of fixing within ourselves concepts about ourselves and tendencies to respond in certain ways in the future. These concepts about ourselves and the tendencies to respond in ways consistent with our self-concepts are at the core of what we are referring to when the term self is used. Since these words first came from others and carried with them the attitudes of these others, now by the repetition of these words, the attitudes of the others toward us have become literally a part of us, of the self.

This cannot be clearly understood unless something of the nature and purpose of language is recognized. Its primitive origins lay in the needs of human beings as they sought to live together. Communication was and is necessary. In our society at the present time, adults view one of their primary responsibilities as being the socialization of the child. Since the ability to communicate greatly facilitates this process, there is pressure to bring the infant along quickly to the place where he can respond to the adult world with what Sullivan refers to as "consensually validated" symbols.[48]

In other words, a particular language is a vital part of and a principle means of conveying a particular culture.

[47] George H. Mead, *Mind, Self, and Society* (Chicago: University of Chicago Press, 1934), p. 108.
[48] Sullivan, *The Interpersonal Theory*, p. 183.

Language is not a passive instrument for the transmission of the ideas of a culture. It itself bears the earmarks of a culture and in turn modifies the character of the situations which it expresses.[49]

So the point is that language not only provides for the accumulation of cultural skills and knowledge as such, but it inevitably passes on to the new generation the ideas, beliefs, values, prejudices, and attitudes of the older generation. "You cannot convey a language as a pure abstraction . . . ; you inevitably in some degree convey also the life that lies behind it." [50] In conforming to the conventions of language behavior, a child also begins to conform to what these conventions imply in his culture. But it is more than merely an outward conformity; these implications (the ideas, beliefs, attitudes, values) become a part of his own private thought, his self, as he "organizes his private thinking along social lines." [51] This process seems to be what Mead has referred to as the "perfecting of the self," in which the child has successfully taken the attitudes and roles of those upon whom he is dependent and made them a vital part of his very own self.[52]

How is this understood as taking place? It can be grasped only as the inseparable linkage of language and personality is seen, as language and selfhood develop together in an interpersonal situation of dependence, as the primary function of language is seen as the establishing of communion between persons and the conveying of self to self.

The answer to the question, "Why does a child learn to talk?", contains insights into the development of the interpersonal self. It is clear that learning to talk grows out of the

---

[49] E. Freeman, *Social Psychology* (New York: Holt, Rinehart & Winston, 1936), p. 106.

[50] Mead, *Mind, Self, and Society*, p. 283.

[51] Cameron, *The Psychology of Behavior Disorders*, p. 86.

[52] Mead, *Mind, Self, and Society*, p. 197.

very intimate relationship of the infant to his parents, particularly to his mother. These are people upon whom he is absolutely dependent, but with whom, at first, he cannot communicate. Within a very brief period of time, however, he cannot help but notice that his cries of distress bring mother to soothe, comfort, and feed. Her responses, then, give a meaning to his own cries, and he has an elementary tool to use to bring about some measure of control over his environment. So gradually these utterances become more consciously intentional.[53] Soon babbling begins, and vocalization becomes one of the infant's chief pleasurable pastimes.[54] But, as we have seen, into this individual activity the parents intrude. The fact that parents want the child to learn to talk must not be overlooked as a factor in learning. This is not alone so that he may be able to communicate his needs more accurately, but it is a matter of pride with them. They imitate his sounds and add simple words of their own. The child then begins to imitate them.

M. M. Lewis states that there are two incentives that impel the child to communicate:

1. Manipulative—To serve his primary needs;
2. Declarative—To express himself.[55]

Perhaps so, but does he not overlook another important factor, the emotional relationship which exists between the child and his parents, and the child's desire to please? The desire to please, of course, is not conscious desire in the adult sense. It is rather the learned response by the infant that certain behavior of his produces behavior on the part of the significant ones that is need-fulfilling for him.

[53] M. M. Lewis, *Language in Society* (New York: Social Science Publishers, 1948), p. 15.
[54] Gardner Murphy, L. B. Murphy, and Theodore Newcomb, *Experimental Social Psychology*, rev. ed. (New York: Harper, 1937), p. 232.
[55] Lewis, *Language in Society*, pp. 23-24.

The parents encourage the child to imitate their sounds. They spend a great amount of time with him. They reward his successful efforts. They respond with gestures of approval and affection to his words or even approximations of words. So what if he does not know what they mean? "Ma-ma-ma" is no different to him than "buh-buh-buh." But it is different to mama. "So if this is what it takes to get this warm, feeding person to love me (*i.e.* feed me and make me comfortable), all right, 'ma-ma-ma.' " And mama, and also "da-da," by their rewarding behavior eliminate the "wrong sounds" and "fixate the right elements." [56] Mowrer quotes John Whiting:

Soon the child is likely to discover that "doing what mama says" is, in general, rewarding and will develop an increasingly strong tendency, at least during the years of dependency, not only to do, but also to say what "mother says." [57]

As the parent conveys himself to the child by meeting the needs of the child, he does so to the accompaniment of language. Then the parent progresses to the teaching of language. Since this takes place during the years of dependency, and since the learning process involves the relationship between the child and significant persons in his life, this whole process necessarily becomes loaded with emotional content, which, we must remember, is the first meaning language has to the child.

Yet, although simple responses of words to words may be explained by imitation and simple conditioning, this alone is not adequate to explain later and more complicated re-

[56] Murphy, *Experimental Social Psychology*, p. 233.

[57] O. H. Mowrer, *Learning Theory and Personality Dynamics* (New York: Ronald Press, 1950), p. 686. [Hereafter cited as Mowrer, *Learning Theory*.]

sponses.[58] This is the relevance of the reference to the obvious emotional involvement. Mowrer, in his highly interesting and informative paper, "On the Psychology of 'Talking Birds,'" after describing the process of teaching birds to talk, says:

Words, as a result of being combined with "loving care," take on alike for bird and baby secondary reinforcing value and . . . they have this value when uttered, not only by others, but also by the bird or baby.[59]

This means that the saying of words begins to be done not just to get an immediate response from the parents, but also because they have begun to be of value in and of themselves.

Identification

Mowrer goes even beyond the concept of the secondary reinforcing value of verbalization to suggest identification as the most dynamic mechanism behind the learning of speech. He says that, according to Freud, intense emotions were at work in this mechanism which would provide a powerful drive or motive. Both liking and fearing are involved. Speech, then, not only results from copied behavior, but from an ambivalent emotional drive to be the person identified with. "The identifier not only acts like but also likes (and fears) the individual identified with." [60]

The emotional content of speech, as we have noted, begins much earlier than the attempts to imitate actual words. It enters when the infant first realizes that his sounds, even though it be crying, bring about some measure of control

[58] Murphy, *Experimental Social Psychology*, p. 232.
[59] Mowrer, *Learning Theory*, pp. 708-9.
[60] *Ibid.*, p. 715.

over significant persons. Even the earliest sounds, as well as the approximation of words and actual words themselves, become a means of establishing and securing a relationship with these significant persons, and thus, these vocalizations are "rooted in affective states." [61] This is the first meaning of words.

Later, as the child is in the process of becoming more articulate, he is doing so at a time when he is meeting his first real frustrations in life, such as weaning, toilet training, not being able to play with everything he puts his hands on. Referring to Mowrer's hypothesis that the child's vocalization now might be an attempt to recapture some of the satisfactions of an earlier period, Percival Symonds adds: "In the frustrating state the infant is afraid of loss or separation and the sounds are an attempt to recapture, at least symbolically, the essence of the mother who is the source of satisfaction." [62] Actually the development of speech now becomes motivated by the attempt to avoid anxiety. It becomes a means of "holding parents, if not physically, at least emotionally near." [63]

Selfhood and language are tied inseparably together. We develop as selves through a process of social interaction in which language plays a determinative role. Our present concepts of ourselves are framed in the thought structures given to us by our language. As we learn language in the context of total dependency upon parents, our learning of words which they give to us places certain emotional attitudes of theirs literally within our self structure. In other words, the interpersonal, highly emotional nature of the situation necessitates

[61] A. R. Lindesmith and A. L. Strauss, *Social Psychology* (New York: Dryden Press, 1949), p. 146.
[62] Mowrer, *Learning Theory*, p. 726.
[63] Murphy, *Experimental Social Psychology*, p. 586.

that the learning of language involves also the incorporation of significant parts of the other self from whom the language is learned. We learn to be social beings, and therefore we are presently sustained as persons through a communion with others which language facilitates, not by means of the simple impartation of information, but through the stimulation of an interpersonal, emotional response.

The developing and sustaining of the interpersonal nature of the self continues because the interpersonal nature of human life continues. "For selfhood to occur and be maintained, a person must be continuing in communication, and the environment must be continuing to accept him as communicator." [64] And the individual, in order to reduce rising gradients of anxiety, to fulfill a growing complexity of needs, continues to identify with, incorporate into himself as a literal part of himself, those aspects of the behavior of others, and thus in reality the others themselves, who are perceived by himself as facilitating the meeting of needs. Erikson points out that "children at different stages of their development identify with those *part aspects* of people by which they themselves are most immediately affected, whether in reality or fantasy." [65] He makes it clear that identity, or selfhood, is not the simple sum of all identifications, but that these introjected "part aspects" of other persons are the material of self formation.

The self seems to have two ways of coming into being in interpersonal relationships, each of which involves the incorporation in some fashion of a significant other person. The first is self-personification, accepting as our proper response to our own being the responses of others to us. The second is

[64] Loomis, *The Self in Pilgrimage*, p. 57.
[65] Erik Erickson, "The Problem of Ego Identity," *Identity and Anxiety*, ed. Maurice Stein, *et. al.* (Glencoe, Ill.: Free Press, 1960), p. 46.

identification with valued attributes of significant others. The first seems to have priority chronologically and forms the elementary self which is necessary before the second can take place.

It has been suggested that what is referred to as the self, although taking place in a unique physiological organism and to some degree directed, modified, and limited by the physiological processes, is actually made up of an individualized organization of the responses of other selves. Macmurray describes it by saying that the development of the individual person is the development of his relation to another person. "Personal individuality is not an original given fact. It is achieved through progressive differentiation of the original unity of the 'you and I.' " [66] The interpersonal situation is not only necessary for the development of such a self, but is also necessary for the sustaining of selfhood.

> The idea of an isolated agent is self-contradictory. Any agent is necessarily in relation to the Other. Apart from this essential relation he does not exist. . . . Persons, therefore, are constituted by their mutual relation to one another.[67]

To understand the self as an interpersonal unity makes it possible to understand anxiety in its interpersonal dimension, and thus to perceive the loss or separation from another, or any threat of separation, as anxiety. That which tends to sever relationship is perceived by the self as danger, as attacking the core of its unified existence. When significant relationship is actually destroyed, a vital part of the self is immediately perceived and experienced as eliminated.

[66] Macmurray, *Persons in Relation*, p. 91.
[67] *Ibid.*, p. 24.

SUMMARY

Each individual self is in reality a social self, or an interpersonal self, comprised of the dynamic union of the learned responses toward one's self whose original source was the perceived behavior of significant others to the infant and small child, and the introjected, perceived significant aspects of emotionally related persons. This process of development is greatly facilitated by the learning of language, which continues to have the same emotional quality about it as did the context of its original learning from significant others. Thus, being a person who came into being through interaction with other persons and whose selfhood is sustained through relationship, any broken relationship is perceived as a threat to the integrity of the self, and the organism responds with the subjective experience of pain and produces behavior which seeks to protect the self.

4

Separation Anxiety in Grief

The preceding discussion of the nature of human personality (that is, each individual self being essentially interpersonal or multipersonal) provides the foundation for understanding precisely what process is activated within a person by the death of someone with whom he has been closely related emotionally. The thesis of this book is that the major dynamic of the inner experience of grief is that of anxiety and that all of the behavioral responses observed and reported in grief are in some way related to this anxiety.

93

To state the understanding of grief in this manner is clearly not to deny that hostility, hate, guilt, depression, and perhaps other emotions which many observers have identified in the reactions of the grieving person are actually involved. They are involved, and they function as complicating factors, perhaps adding to the intensity of the subjective experience, very likely making grief work more difficult. Yet one of the values of defining grief in terms of anxiety is the possibility of perceiving the close dynamic relationship between these other emotional responses and the central affect itself.

In this chapter, the attempt will be made to present as clearly as possible the source of the pain which is felt and which has been termed anxiety, and to do so in such a way as to make clear that the experience of the death of an emotionally significant person is simply one, albeit an extremely intense one, in a series of experiences which are psychodynamically the same. These are termed separation experiences, and anxiety itself is defined as fear of separation.

BASIC ANXIETY: ORIGIN AND NATURE

The concept of basic anxiety is a useful one. It implies a number of things. First, it points to the original experience or experiences of anxiety upon which all other later anxiety reactions are based, no matter how these may be stimulated nor what terminology be used to describe them.

The second implication is that of the universal learning of anxiety. There are various ways of expressing this. We have already discussed Freud's concept of the intrapsychic origin of anxiety. Yet it is more useful for our purposes to follow the new directions toward which he seemed to be pointing and which Whitaker and Malone summarize by saying that

that which becomes *intra*personal was originally *inter*personal.[1]

Horney speaks of basic anxiety as being the infant's response to "the feeling . . . of being isolated and helpless in a potentially hostile world." [2] Being inherently dependent upon others, this feeling may be either lessened or increased by parental behavior which is warm, loving, need fulfilling or which is erratic and lacking in these attitudes.

Sullivan observed that anxiety is unavoidably perpetuating from one generation to the next, since it is a response which is made by the infant to the anxious mother, who is perceived by the infant as threatening his security. It is learned simply by empathy.[3]

Garre confirms Sullivan's view that anxiety is unavoidably present in every human existence.[4] This is in contrast with other animal life. First, the energy of the parent is not instinctively directed toward the small child; it can be diverted into other channels. Therefore, the more energy which is bound to the past the less is available to the child in the present and future. Second, humans have interpretations and emotions (including fear, disgust, reluctance) in regard to reproduction. To the degree that the negative emotions are present, the child is seen as a burden and is unwanted. To the degree that the child is an unwanted burden, there is resentment on the part of the parent and the wish to be rid of the child. The child, on the emotional level "will be pervaded by the feeling that its existence is threatened. It will

[1] Carl Whitaker and Thomas P. Malone, "Anxiety and Psychotherapy," *Identity and Anxiety,* pp. 167-68.
[2] Karen Horney, *Our Inner Conflicts* (New York: W. W. Norton, 1945), p. 41.
[3] Sullivan, *The Interpersonal Theory,* p. 41.
[4] Walter J. Garre, *Basic Anxiety* (New York: Philosophical Library, 1962), pp. 1-4.

fear death to the degree that it senses its mother's resentment. We should not underrate the infant's perceptivity." [5]

A final contribution of the concept of basic anxiety is that it points to anxiety as being a central motivating force for the human organism, a drive calling for the learning of habitual responses which form a large part of individual personality. It is recognized that anxiety (threat, psychic pain) must be overcome or avoided and that forms of behavior are developed in order to cope with it. Garre says that "basic anxiety is the key to personality adjustment, . . . the central point in the adaptation of humans to life." [6] The behavior which is learned is in relation to others, since personality is structured and organized out of affective states within the matrix of interpersonal relationships. [7]

All theories of anxiety seem to hold in common a number of ideas. Anxiety is essentially the perception of a threat to the self; some internal or external event or situation is interpreted on an unconscious level as a danger. There are elements both of the past and future. The stimulus triggers a memory of a past threatening situation, and as a result pain to the self is anticipated. Avoidance of this danger, or threat, is sought by some form of escape from or denial or distortion of the perceived situation.

WHAT IS FEARED?

The major question is, "What is it that is feared, and why?" If we answer the question in terms of separation from another, it must still be asked, "Why is separation feared?" Answers in terms of instinct have already been portrayed as not being

[5] *Ibid.,* p. 2.
[6] *Ibid.,* pp. 3-4.
[7] Whitaker and Malone, "Anxiety and Psychotherapy," pp. 167-68.

helpful in understanding either the origin or the contemporary meaning of the reaction.[8]

Separation Fear as a Response Conditioned by Pain

The attempt at an explanation must begin with a very simple, ridiculously self-evident statement: pain is painful. When the infant and his very first experiences are considered, great care must be taken not to read into his behavior the adult meanings of certain responses to specific stimuli. It cannot legitimately be said that the infant is first afraid of separation from a significant other, or of death, or even that he is afraid in the meaning that it will later come to have. The infant, as far as adults can judge, simply has a global response to pleasure and pain, comfort and discomfort, and he responds to pain or discomfort by the automatic mechanism of crying. Heibrunn makes the observation which any mother could have made, that her leaving the room provokes crying in the baby. The reason given is the infant's fear of abandonment and annihilation.[9] Perhaps this fear develops later, but it is not present at first. The meaning of abandonment has to be learned. The infant is helpless. But he does not at first "know" himself to be helpless. He needs another person in order to live. Grotjahn points out the significance of the infant's fear of being left alone by the mother, a separation which could lead to his death.[10] But it must not be assumed that the infant at first has some knowledge of this or even that he "knows" it or has some intuition of it on an unconscious level. If actually left unattended, he would soon die. In this case he would not learn

[8] See pp. 75-78.
[9] Gert Heibrunn, "On Weeping," *Psychoanalytic Quarterly*, XXIV (1955), 252.
[10] Martin Grotjahn, "Ego Identity and the Fear of Death and Dying," *Journal of the Hillside Hospital*, IX (1960), 148.

or "know" anything; he would not know anxiety as people can later experience it and communicate their experiences of it. He would have only the global, physiological response to displeasure, discomfort, pain, without even a primitive, unconscious interpretation of anxiety. As this pain grows more and more intense a response can be observed which adults could describe as panic, a global, unthinking response.

However, the minute anything is done to relieve pain, to bring pleasure (to feed, to warm, to dry, to powder), learning begins to take place which changes the entire picture. The infant learns to become dependent upon and to seek mothering behavior. He learns that there are experiences other than pain. He learns that he is helpless to change the experience from pain to comfort, except insofar as the automatic response of crying is rewarded by comforting, mothering behavior and is thus stamped in as social behavior, a form of behavior which elicits a response from another. Monsour has spoken of the infant's "crying as a symbol of need-distress . . . which summons the mother into symbiosis." [11] When the mothering one is present, he has now learned to anticipate the meeting of his needs. When the other is not present, his needs are frustrated and pain and discomfort are felt. There is the learned interpretation that the absence of the mothering one is a threat to his well-being. Or, he may have learned that when the significant other is present his needs are sometimes met and sometimes not met. Still, by virtue of the fact that he is kept alive, there is a learned dependence on the mother. Yet along with this there is also a learned uncertainty concerning the meeting of his needs, and thus the interpretation of possible threat to his comfort and satisfaction even in the presence of the mother. However, the only alternative the infant has is to cling to the

[11] Karem J. Monsour, "Asthma and the Fear of Death" *Psychoanalytic Quarterly*, XXIX (1960), 66.

Separation Anxiety in Grief

only object of possible satisfaction offered to him by his environment. "Intolerable anxiety (is) helplessly accepted as part of the relationship with the mother." [12] So either way, whether the mother is regularly need fulfilling and anxiety reducing or whether she is anxious and inadequate and frustrating and herself a threat, the presence and approval of the significant other is learned by the infant as that which must be sought and sustained and absence and disapproval is perceived as a prelude to frustration and pain. Because of "remembered" pain in contrast with comfort, there is the learned anticipated pain and discomfort, the threat to his well-being.

Thus it is seen that the infant has learned of his own helplessness; he has learned to depend on others; he has learned to fear the absence of the significant other. In other words, the uninterpreted, global experience of pain contrasted with the experience of comfort forms the foundation for the learning of anxiety, the learned, perceived threat to the self, with the interpretation of the intensity of the threat in relation to one's perceived ability or lack of it to cope with the danger situation.

Evidence from experimental psychology. Substantiation of this approach is found in the work of experimental psychologists. Hoch states:

The perception of pain, and related experiences, must be thought of as precursors to the development of fear and anxiety. . . . Fear reactions in the beginning are unconditioned responses and produce a total reaction of the organism in preparation to fight or flight as the environmental constellation demands it.[13]

[12] *Ibid.*
[13] Paul H. Hoch, "Biosocial Aspects of Anxiety," *Anxiety,* ed. Paul H. Hoch and Joseph Zubin (New York: Grune & Stratton, 1950), p. 106.

The only oversight of this statement is that it is not complete in regard to the human infant, who can neither fight nor flee as forms of direct, overt behavior, and who is totally dependent upon the type and quality of care the mothering person or persons desire to give and are capable of giving.

Mowrer has also stated the experimentalist's understanding of the origin of fear:

Closely associated with the capacity to feel pain and other primary drives is the capacity to feel fear. . . . Laboratory studies indicate that in its most primitive, unconditioned forms, fear is aroused by pain and other forms of intense stimulation; whereas, in its conditioned or learned form, it is set off by those inherently harmless stimuli which happen to have been temporally associated, or contiguous, with pain producing objects or events. Elicited originally, along with pain, by noxious stimulation, fear is subsequently produced in pure form by *signals.*[14]

It is to be noted that in this view it is clear that anxiety is based upon a somatic condition of pain, or increased tension. Now this is precisely what Freud has pointed to in his first theory as the source of anxiety: increased tension, to which he applied the term sexual, which did not have a channel of expression and thereby of reduction. However, the viewpoint being presented here has picked up the insights later given, but not fully worked out, by Freud and which have also been pointed to by other observers. This viewpoint insists on the origin of anxiety out of the physiological condition of pain, not necessarily specifically localized pain, but a general sense of discomfort, the loss of the global sense of well-being. Yet

[14] O. H. Mowrer, "Pain, Punishment, and Anxiety," *Anxiety,* pp. 33-34.

this position goes further to indicate that this internal condition is only the starting point for the learning of an anxiety which can best be described by saying that it is the fear of separation from the significant other upon whose presence the organism's well-being depends. Or, stated another way, it is the concern for one's own well-being which is threatened by the absence of the mothering one.

At this point the infant does not have an internalized ego. One of two things, or perhaps both of two things, could be said. If the infant has an ego, it is simply the physiological organism as such. On the other hand, Schur makes a provocative reference to the mother as the infant's external ego.[15] This concept is quite compatible with the ideas being presented here.

It has been shown in the previous chapter that the responses of significant others toward the infant are incorporated as his attitude toward himself, and thus is the foundation of the self. The external ego, the mother, gradually becomes internalized: not only her loving and accepting behavior, but also her punishing and disapproving behavior, which includes her leaving, removing her presence, the experiences of her absence. So built into the organization of affective responses which we call the self, derived from and to a large degree equivalent to the mother, is the fear of her absence, the anxiety which results from separation from her. These are the good and bad objects that Klein spoke of, now having become the "good me" and "bad me" that Sullivan described. An individual's self contains within it the tendency to respond to separation from significant others as if it were a threat to the existence of the self, experienced as the signal of anxiety.

[15] Max Schur, "Discussion," *The Psychoanalytic Study of the Child*, XV (1960), 77.

Summary of the learning sequence. Let us summarize now the development of the hypothesis to this point: first is pain; second is the fear of pain, anticipation of it; third is the fear of the absence of the mothering one which signals that pain is to come; fourth, the development of the ego through the internalization of the other, including the "leaving," threatening behavior of the mother; fifth, the perception of separation from significant others as threat to the self. It is now only a short step to the first inarticulated, and later perhaps conscious and expressed, fear of the annihilation of the ego, the loss of identity, the ceasing to be as a person, self-loss. Finally, when it is learned through experience, there is the fear of death which is perceived to be the final and total destruction of identity.

Thus, it is to be seen that the fear of separation is grounded in the cumulative learning experiences of the infant, beginning immediately after birth but taking some unspecified time for development, that absence of the mothering one tends to be temporally congruous with an increase of somatic tension, pain, discomfort, and the return of the mother tends to bring the rewarding behavior of reduction of tension, comfort. The resultant learning is that separation from the significant other is to be feared, and the presence of the other is to be sought as if the other were identical with one's own self.

Fear of the Loss of One's Self Through Separation

The answer to the question, "What is feared in the anxiety reaction?" is, on the level of the older child, the adolescent, the adult, that it is the destruction of one's own self, or death. Simmel said that since the ego's aim is to maintain itself, the basic fear is of annihilation, of death.[16] Meissner stated that

[16] Ernst Simmel, "Self-Preservation and the Death Instinct," *Psychoanalytic Quarterly*, XIII (1944), 165-66.

what the person dreads is the dissolution of his own personality.[17] The point is clear enough. This is the ultimate dread on the level of one who has moved through all of the stages of learning presented above. But that which because of this early learning cues off the perception of threat to one's own self, one's very life as a person, is separation from the significant other person, broken or disrupted relationships. Therefore when the term anxiety is used, it should be conceived of as separation fear.

Not only does the self come into being in the context of affective interpersonal relationships and take on a basically interpersonal nature itself to such a degree that the loss of or separation from a significant person by the infant or small child is perceived to be a threat to its own well-being, but the adult human continues to have his self or ego needs met through meaningful relations with others. Man does not live alone, and indeed cannot without changing the nature of the self. Moreno goes so far as to say that the smallest social unit is what he calls the "social atom," this being "simply an individual and the people (near or distant) to whom he is emotionally related at the time." [18] Therefore, the removal of some person from the social atom is experienced as a threat to the individual who is the nucleus of that atom. "A man dies when his social atom dies." [19] Broken relationship is thus a stimulus to the ego's learned response to separation as threat, or anxiety.

May's conclusion has emphasized anxiety as the behavioral response signaling avoidance to any situation which is perceived as involving danger to one's existence as a self, "the

[17] W. W. Meissner, "Affective Response to Psychoanalytic Death Symbols," *Journal of Abnormal and Social Psychology*, LVI (1958), 295.
[18] J. L. Moreno, "The Social Atom and Death," *Sociometry*, X (1947), 80.
[19] *Ibid.*, p. 84.

apprehension cued off by a threat to some value which the individual holds essential to his existence as a personality." [20]

The Central Value to One's Self of Relation with the Other

The interpersonal theory of personality development and dynamics holds that the major value in one's existence as a person is his relationship with other persons. This has been articulated in the previous chapter by seeking to show that the infant learns to be a self only by incorporation of and identification with other persons, although it has been noted that there are cultural differences in the kind, number, and intensity of identifications. His own being can never even be conceived of apart from relation with others. Therefore a threat to the relationship is always perceived as a threat to the self. There is no escape by any person from "what is for him the ultimate threat to his existence—isolation from the Other by the act of the Other." [21]

The other as a major value in a person's life is presented in the perceptive view of Fromm-Reichmann:

The conception of anxiety as the expression of the anticipated loss of love and approval, or separation, social isolation, or disruption of one's interpersonal relationships implies its close psychological affinity to loneliness. In fact, I believe that many of the emotional states to which psychiatrists refer as anxiety are actually states of loneliness or fear of loneliness.[22]

One is reminded of the "terror" of loneliness as it is so poignantly described by Moustakas out of his own experience: "No one fully understood my terror or how this terror gave

[20] May, *The Meaning of Anxiety*, p. 191.

[21] Macmurray, *Persons in Relation*, p. 89.

[22] Frieda Fromm-Reichmann, "Psychiatric Aspects of Anxiety," *Identity and Anxiety*, p. 132.

impetus to deep feelings of loneliness and isolation which had lain dormant within me." [23] Later he speaks of "loneliness anxiety" and the "vague, diffuse fear of loneliness." [24]

Relationship with others in a situation of mutual investment of affection is the central value of human life as it is known in this and many other cultures. A threat to that value is a threat to our own being; the perception of that threat cues the signal of anxiety, and the organism responds with behavioral mechanisms of defense. This behavior has as its purpose the evasion, denial, or distortion of reality in such a way as to reduce the perception of threat to the self, and includes repression, denial, phantasy, emotional insulation, apathy, substitution or displacement, rationalization, regression, projection, reaction formation, identification, compensation, sublimation. In addition there are overt attempts at escape through withdrawal, exaggerated activity, intensified sexual life, the use of drugs, and even escape into illness.

SEPARATION ANXIETY AS THE CENTRAL DYNAMIC OF GRIEF

In the light of the definition of anxiety as being essentially the fear response to separation from a significant other and the universal recognition of grief as a broken human relationship, an unusually dramatic and seemingly permanent form of loss of or separation from one in whom a person has emotional investment and with whom he has identified to some degree, the conclusion seems inescapable that at the very center of grief is separation anxiety. Grief is one among many of a lifetime of separation experiences, each stimulating reactions

[23] Clark E. Moustakas, *Loneliness* (New York: Prentice-Hall, 1961), p. 2.
[24] *Ibid.*, pp. 25-26.

of anxiety, differing in intensity because of a variety of factors, yet all being of basically the same order. Since the self is made up of a series of identifications, of emotional investments, then the destruction of the external referent is perceived and experienced as the destruction of an important aspect of one's own selfhood. Could any clearer and more potent illustration be found of separation from or the absence of an emotionally significant other person than the event of his death? The death of this other cues the response, threat to self, anxiety.

Evidence for the Thesis

Evidence for this conclusion comes from several sources. First, personal reports of grief sufferers themselves have indicated the similarities of the subjective experience. Second, empirical data of psychotherapists relate the responses of grief and anxiety. Third, when the behavioral reactions of grief and anxiety are isolated, their identity can be observed.

Personal reports. C. S. Lewis is an example, writing following the death of his wife: "No one ever told me that grief felt so much like fear." [25] A personal report to the writer by a woman whose husband had died after an illness states: "There was a feeling of anxiety before his passing. After, I seemed in a state of shock, a daze." And later: "I was afraid: Do not know why, unless it was because I always felt so secure with my husband."

In many cases bereavement dreams are not distinguishable from anxiety dreams. A man whose wife was suffering from a terminal illness reported a series of nightmares after which he woke up with characteristic signs of anxiety. In one dream

[25] C. S. Lewis, *A Grief Observed* (New York: Seabury Press, 1963), p. 7.

his wife would be dying or dead. In another dream the subject would be dying by choking, suffocating. In yet another dream, upon awakening he would be unable to determine clearly whether it was he or his wife who was dying in the dream. In these cases the dreams tell more clearly and more dramatically than any written statement the fact that the death of an emotionally significant other is perceived by the ego as its own death, and that the subjective experience and its physiological accompaniments are those of the outbreak into consciousness of anxiety.

The strength of anxiety in grief and the thesis of Deutsch that the affect of "unmanifested grief will be found expressed to the full in one way or the other," [26] was demonstrated in the case of a college girl referred for counseling. She had been having occasional depressions with crying, outcroppings of mild anxiety, vague uneasiness and restlessness and dissatisfaction. It was not difficult for her to link these reactions intellectually to the deaths of her father, mother, and sister in an automobile accident when she was driving. But why anxiety and depression almost two years later? She had received multiple serious injuries from the accident and had been in the hospital for several months, actually out of touch with the reality of the situation for weeks, unable to attend the funeral, with total attention taken up with her own pain and disability. When finally she left the hospital, she was "accustomed" to the separation, and full grieving had never been accomplished. The effect of the grief was now being expressed and experienced as overt anxiety and depression.

The reality of anxiety in grief is a conclusion that can be reached because of various types of reports from and observations of grief sufferers themselves.

[26] Deutsch, "Absence of Grief," p. 13.

107

Evidence from psychotherapy. Second, there is strong cumulative evidence from the observations of therapists. Deutsch has spoken of the replacement of normal mourning by a state of severe anxiety in neurotic patients.[27] This could logically be interpreted as being simply the adding of anxiety to anxiety, separation fear cued off by the death of an emotionally related person laid upon a person who already operated at a high level of anxiety. Deutsch saw grief as attacking the integrity of the ego, one response to which is regression to infantile anxiety,[28] which, of course, in its signal effect is precisely the same perception, threat to the ego.

Anderson follows this same line of thought, defining anxiety as the ego's signal of threat to its existence, and going on to say that the ego incorporates into itself that which threatens it and that for which it mourns. Absence of the object of value equals anxiety; it also equals grief.[29] Whether called grief or anxiety, it matters not; when the affect is expressed overtly it is an anxiety state.

Klein actually identifies anxiety and grief by simply calling the separation experiences of the infant which others have termed anxiety, "infantile mourning," and stating that adult mourning can be understood as a reproduction of analogous separation experiences.[30] The death of a loved person is the stimulus reactivating earlier experiences of separation which are now experienced as present threats.[31] Grief and anxiety, according to her, are identical experiences of separation fear.

Bowlby makes the most emphatic statement of all growing

[27] *Ibid.*
[28] *Ibid.,* p. 16.
[29] Charles Anderson, "Aspects of Pathological Grief and Mourning," *International Journal of Psychoanalysis,* XXX (1949), 49-50.
[30] Klein, "Mourning and Its Relation to Manic-Depressive States," p. 126.
[31] *Ibid.,* p. 136.

out of his clinical work: "Separation anxiety, grief and mourning, and defense are phases of a single process." [32] There seems to be no difference between separation from the mother on the part of the child and the separation by the death of an emotionally significant person on the part of an adult.[33] Bowlby feels that the child's separation anxiety ought clearly to be designated by its true name of grief. Absence and death are identical psychic experiences for a person.[34]

This conclusion concerning the identity of anxiety and grief seems to be demonstrated by a woman who sought counseling during the first few months following her divorce. She reported feelings of depression, self-doubt, and guilt; periods of shakiness, uncontrollable crying, and anxiety. Since the conditions of the marriage had been, from her description, utterly intolerable in a number of ways for many years, one might well expect a sense of relief and release to be the predominant responses to the divorce. She herself seemed to have had this expectation, and therefore could not understand these present feelings. Treating this as a crisis situation, an acute sense of threat to the self cued off by the divorce, the therapist pursued the procedure of seeking similar reactions from the past in order both to bring insight into the nature of the present experience and in order to make an inventory of problem-solving resources. The woman's response of insight was almost immediate, "Why, I felt just like this when my baby died only a few months after birth." The affective reactions to the drastic separation of the death of one with whom she had identified herself were now being reproduced in the experience of the separation of divorce, in the midst of which she was conscious of anxiety as a major force.

[32] Bowlby, "Grief and Mourning in Infancy and Childhood," p. 9.
[33] *Ibid.*, p. 10.
[34] *Ibid.*, p. 16.

Identity of behavioral responses. A third reason for stating that the anxiety state is central in grief is because behavioral reactions to both can be isolated and seen as essentially the same.

The purpose of the psychological defense or adjustive mechanisms to anxiety has been stated as that of reducing the painful affect of anxiety by denying or distorting reality in some way. These same mechanisms can be seen operating in grief in the same manner toward the same end.

Anderson stated in the context of his apparent identifying of anxiety and grief that just as in the former, some people develop neurotic and even psychotic symptoms when the intense affect of morbid grief has not been abreacted.[35]

Fulcomer in his thorough cataloging of the behavior of the grief-stricken has observed apathy and emotional insulation or detachment, depression, self-blame, projection of blame onto others, displaced hostility, identification with the role and/or characteristics of the deceased, repression of affect, phantasy involving an idealized image of the other and the relationship which existed, sublimation through activity in groups and causes, substitution of relationships.[36]

Fulcomer's observations are corroborated by Eliot, who has reported a rejection of reality, a sense of unreality, detachment, repression, self-blame, projection, compensation, rationalization, identification with the deceased, transference, and substitution.[37] Lindemann also spoke of observing an activated phantasy life concerning the deceased, displaced hostility, identification, a sense of unreality, emotional distance from others,

[35] Anderson, "Aspects of Pathological Grief and Mourning," p. 49.
[36] Fulcomer, "The Adjustive Behavior," pp. 87-159.
[37] Eliot, "The Bereaved Family," *Annals of the American Academy of Political and Social Science,* CLX (1932), pp. 185-86.

and an apathy so great as to appear to be almost schizophrenic in nature.[38]

As indicated earlier, Deutsch has mentioned regression as one of the mechanisms of defense, but showing that regression takes one back to infantile anxiety.[39] The adult is no longer a child, but part of the child is in every adult. It has already been explained how helplessness is learned by the infant in the situation of increased pain in the absence of the mothering one. The adult who is confronted by the death of an emotionally significant person has the experience of total frustration and helplessness to fulfill the desire to sustain the physical presence of the deceased. So the same separation anxiety, the perception of one's helplessness in the face of threat to the self, of which the infant's first separation experiences were the prototype, is set off. Yet one response to contemporary anxieties is to escape to the security patterns of earlier years, regression.

The question arises as to whether this is not perhaps the first mechanism that usually operates in grief-anxiety, with the subsequent overt behavior and mechanisms being a reflection of the earlier security patterns of that particular person: apathy, withdrawal, identification, phantasy.

Also, in view of the fact that death means the removal of the physical presence of an emotionally meaningful person, would not regression mean reverting to the behavior of the child which he utilized to hold the significant other near, namely, talking? In chapter 3 it was seen that language was learned in a highly emotionally charged interpersonal situation in such a way that the learning to speak words was temporally contiguous with the process of identification with the parents. It was concluded that one of the meanings of the child's verbal-

[38] Lindemann, "Symptomatology," pp. 9-10, 12-15.
[39] Deutsch, "Absence of Grief," p. 16.

izing was his sense of maintaining the strength of his own ego by drawing and holding the parents near. The words were the substitution for presence; emotionally they meant the same.

Orlansky has said that talking is a way of relieving anxiety.[40] This is a rather common observation. But outside of being a form of physical activity which does literally relieve physical tension, why should it relieve anxiety? Orlansky states that it is because of its social meaning.[41] It is true that one of the major needs of the grief-stricken is social intercourse, communication, but this is not the first conscious purpose of talking at the time of bereavement. The concept of holding the significant other emotionally near at a time when separation takes place or is threatened is the key. Increased talking has been reported as a response in the situation of grief not only by Orlansky, but also by Lindemann,[42] with the interpretation that communication of remembered experiences with the deceased is the emotional equivalent of reliving them.[43]

After the tension of anxiety is relieved, and even while the process is going on, of course, the regressive tendency of talking is also the means of maintaining contemporary relationships and establishing new ones, which is ultimately necessary for the healing of grief and reentering life.

Other than the mental mechanisms and their resulting behavior, several writers have included other forms of overt behavior as responses of grief. Talking as an act of tension reduction has already been discussed in relation to regression, and it was earlier suggested that perhaps any response to grief-

[40] Orlansky, "Reactions to the Death of President Roosevelt," pp. 233, 254.

[41] *Ibid.*, p. 253.

[42] Lindemann, "Symptomatology," p. 10.

[43] Lloyd E. Foster, *et al.*, "Grief," *Pastoral Psychology*, I (June, 1950), 30.

anxiety which is observed is a regressive behavior pattern. Hypomania as a global response has also been observed, almost continuous and, on the whole, meaningless activity and excitement.[44] The direct action of escape from the situation through withdrawal, social isolation, is also common.[45]

Other aspects of overt behavior are the physical responses in the first reaction to grief which are those which are also noted in an acute anxiety attack: not only crying, but tightening of the throat, sensation of a load on one's chest, disturbances of breathing such as gulping, gasping, sighing, the feeling of suffocating; inability to eat, no appetite, food seeming to stick in the throat; frequent excitation of bowels and kidneys; either physical exhaustion or agitation.[46]

Two forms of illness often seem to result from grief just as they do from anxiety. A third form might even be noted as a possibility. One of these is neurotic in nature and the second is psychosomatic. The former is the result of the mechanism of identification, in which the dynamics of this mechanism, already operating in the relationship, are intensified by the increased anxiety brought about by the separation by death, and the bereaved begins to exhibit symptoms related to the final illness of the deceased.[47] Cases of this nature have been reported by Brewster, who reports the case of a woman who developed shortness of breath and a feeling of suffocation following her brother's death,[48] and Creegan, who presented the case of the boy who, following the death of his mother,

---

[44] Fulcomer, "The Adjustive Behavior," pp. 105, 119; Lindemann, "Symptomatology," p. 10; Bowlby, "Grief and Mourning in Early Infancy and Childhood," p. 19.

[45] Eliot, "The Bereaved Family," p. 186; Lindemann, "Symptomatology," p. 14.

[46] Lindemann, "Symptomatology," p. 9.

[47] *Ibid.*, p. 10.

[48] Brewster, "Grief: A Disrupted Human Relationship," p. 116.

expressed his repressed hostility toward her by killing his dog
and then sought to resolve the guilt and grief by identification
with her in the form of psychogenic heart attacks.[49]

Another illustration of the mechanism of identification is the
instance of a male college student who went to a counselor
because of his distress over his frequent inability to get his
breath. He reported the feeling of suffocating, sometimes relatively mild but not infrequently to the point of panic. His
father had been dead some eight years at the time, but the
young man still remembered visiting his sick bed a few times
during a lingering illness, at which time the father had had
breathing difficulties. The symptoms of the student began to
clear up when after about two months of counseling he spent
all of two consecutive sessions weeping, with deep, body-rack-
ing sobs and deep sighing, as he recounted and now relived
feelings toward his father.

The second form of illness which can be seen occasionally
rising out of grief-anxiety is psychosomatic, or psychophysiological. This differs from the first in that in psychophysiological
illness there is actual organ pathology. Both Garre and Engel
have briefly laid the groundwork for this understanding of
illness, the former in relation to a discussion of anxiety, the
latter in a discussion of grief. Garre has pointed out that
anxiety as such is intolerable to human experience, and that
the affect constantly seeks to be converted into a more bearable
form. Somatic illness is one of these.[50] He later mentions
colitis specifically as a reaction to anxiety, which is to be
thought of as fear of abandonment.[51] Lindemann, too, has
singled out colitis as an illustration of a psychosomatic illness
related to grief. In a study of forty-one patients with the dis-

[49] Creegan, "A Symbolic Action During Bereavement," pp. 403-5.
[50] Garre, *Basic Anxiety*, p. 5.
[51] *Ibid.*, p. 8.

order, he noted that thirty-three of them had developed the disease closely following the loss of an emotionally significant person.[52] Stern has discovered in an investigation of grief in later life that among the elderly there is a tendency to exhibit fewer of certain other types of symptoms but that there is a preponderance of somatic illness.[53] As a physician, Engel has observed the occurrence of grief immediately preceding illness, and he has declared that this ought not to be thought of as coincidental.[54]

The third form of illness which might well be related to the grief reaction, as it is also suggested as a possible consequence of intense anxiety, is physiogenic (organic) illness, in which the grief-anxiety plays at least a preconditioning role. Garre said that anxiety ought not to be overlooked as an influential factor in lowering the body's resistance to germs and viruses.[55] Engel states it in relation to grief, saying that it is possible that biochemical or physiological processes associated with grief may become the condition for more serious somatic changes.[56]

Perhaps more than coincidentally the young college man cited above as exhibiting identification with the symptoms of his dead father contracted tuberculosis within a year or so after the death of his father. The disease was thoroughly arrested within the year, and it was then that the symptoms of breathing disturbances arose, with one medical examination after another failing to find any further organic pathology.

Just as ego defense mechanisms, overt behavior of escape and tension reduction, physical symptoms, and even illness are seen as reactions to anxiety with a view to the reduction

---

[52] Lindemann, "Symptomatology," p. 13.
[53] Karl Stern, *et al.*, "Grief Reactions in Later Life," *American Journal of Psychiatry*, CVIII (1951), 289.
[54] Engel, "Is Grief a Disease?" pp. 20-21.
[55] Garre, *Basic Anxiety*, p. 5.
[56] Engel, "Is Grief a Disease?" p. 21.

of the subjective experience of pain following an early learned pattern of pain avoidance, so also should many of the behavioral responses of the bereaved be understood as defenses against perceived threats to the ego.

SUMMARY

The thesis that separation anxiety is the core experience and the major dynamic element in grief has been developed by seeking to elaborate the infant's learning to fear the absence of the mothering one, beginning with his global experience of pain, discomfort, increased tension, broken by experiences of comfort and satisfaction when the significant other is present and mothering behavior is being performed. The absence of the mother is learned to be the equivalent of the anticipation of increased tension, pain, that has been experienced and is now remembered, because of the infant's learned sense of helplessness and dependence. This becomes the prototype experience whose painful affect is triggered by continuing experiences of separation from significant others. The central value of meaningful relationships with others as a means of sustaining one's own being is learned in this interpersonal matrix. To be separated from emotionally important persons is perceived as a threat to the self. This is anxiety, a separation fear.

Perhaps the best summary of the total process involved in the situations of separation anxiety and grief which lead to the conclusion that grief cannot be understood apart from an analysis of anxiety has been made by Bowlby, whose observations were reported in chapter 2. The responses to both separation from the mother by the child and loss of a loved object through death by an adult included self-blame (guilt), displaced hostility, appeals for help (frequently accompanied by the rejection of offers of aid), withdrawal, despair, regression, inertia, sense of emptiness, loss of organized social patterns of activity, but finally with the reorganization of behavior directed toward a new object.[57]

The reasons, then, for declaring the proposition that acute anxiety reaction is the major dynamic factor in grief and that much of the experiences and behavior noted in grief are in the same category as the various attempted defenses against and escape from anxiety are: first, the subjective experiences are reported to be the same by many who have undergone them; second, the formulations of therapists, who have had clinical experience with the separation anxiety of children and who have worked with children and adults in grief, identify the two as being essentially the same; and third, the mechanisms of defense, the behavior of escape and avoidance, the physical symptoms, and other behavior accompanying and following the two can be recognized as the same in form and purpose.

[57] Bowlby, "Grief and Mourning in Early Infancy and Childhood," pp. 17-20.

5

Guilt, Hostility, and Grief

It would be difficult to add any original insights to the rather massive accumulation of literature dealing with guilt. In addition, as one reviews the material concerning grief that has been published, it is noted that guilt and grief are frequently related. However, in expressing this relationship, it has not been clearly and explicitly stated that guilt itself is a form of anxiety, although this idea is common enough in other psychological and psychotherapeutic literature.

The relation of guilt to grief has been understood in one of two ways, depending upon the definition of grief itself. Where grief was assumed to be a term applied to a complex of several interacting emotions occasioned by the death of a person to whom one has been emotionally related, guilt was simply listed as one of the several possible emotions which combined to produce a total affect. Where grief was spoken of in such a way that it seemed to be a separate and distinguishable emotion *per se,* guilt was discussed, usually along with hostility, as being an additional emotion which was operating as a complicating factor in the situation.

The purpose of this chapter is merely to point out that guilt as a form of anxiety is reinforcing to the separation anxiety of grief. Therefore when guilt and grief are discussed in relation to one another, the meaning is that of anxiety added to anxiety, and that guilt also has its origin in a separation fear. It would be important, too, to clarify in some detail the precise way in which hostility, which has frequently been observed as being expressed in the grief situation, is involved in the generation of the guilt feelings of the bereaved person.

GUILT AS MORAL ANXIETY

Sigmund Freud

Freud laid the groundwork for the understanding of guilt as anxiety. The super-ego is described as coming into being as a result of the growing intensity of the male child's object-cathexis of the mother and his perception of his father as an obstacle to his sexual wishes. The earlier identification with the father now includes in it the desire to get rid of him, creating an ambivalent relation. The resolution of this complex should ordinarily take place through increased identification with the father. At the same time there is also an element of identification with the mother and some ambivalence toward her. The general outcome of this situation is the forming of an aspect of the ego, the super-ego, which consists of some combination of these two identifications.[1] This is the source of feelings of guilt, the criticism of the ego by the super-ego. When the latter is particularly severe, its condemnation of the ego is quite painful and the ego responds with repression. As a matter of fact, much guilt must ordinarily remain unconscious because of its origin in the Oedipus complex, which is unconscious.[2]

The nature of this guilt is no different from any other threat which the ego perceives. There is danger from the external world, from the strength of the id, and from the severity of the ego. "Three kinds of anxiety correspond to these three dangers, since anxiety is the expression of a retreat from danger." [3] In the same way that a danger from the outside seems to threaten the existence of the ego, so the strong super-ego is also perceived as an annihilating force, the response to which is fear, anxiety, which in this latter case is called guilt. In the midst of the Oedipus situation the major fear of the child is that of castration by the father, the higher being. With the internalization of the father there is also the introjection of his punishing behavior of castration. This forms the affective nucleus—dread of castration—which continues as fear of conscience, or guilt.[4]

Freud goes on to make a significant comment concerning the ego: "To the ego, therefore, living means the same as being loved." [5] This includes being loved by the super-ego in the

[1] Standard Edition, XIX, 31-34.
[2] *Ibid.*, pp. 51-52.
[3] *Ibid.*, p. 56.
[4] *Ibid.*, p. 57.
[5] *Ibid.*, p. 58.

same way that it meant being loved by the mother and father prior to their internalization. Thus, the severe criticism of the ego has the same meaning as castration, the withdrawal of the loving support of the significant persons at a time of dependence upon them.

Here, moreover, is once again the same situation as that which underlay the first great anxiety—state of birth and the infantile anxiety of longing for an absent person—the anxiety of separation from the protecting mother.[6]

So Freud has come to the point of saying that in the person in whom there operates some level of anxiety, the fear of separation from the significant other, there is the dynamic, affective residue of another experience where separation has been threatened, the Oedipal situation. Fear of the super-ego in this case is called guilt. It is also a separation anxiety, of the same nature as anxiety in its original experiences. He goes on to make more explicit the concept of separation contained in the formulation of feelings of guilt as an extension of the punishment of castration by showing that the value of the penis grows out of the child's primitive understanding that it is the organ which he needs in order to obtain union with the mother, therefore its loss is perceived as separation from her.[7]

One other important aspect of the dynamics of the super-ego is the perception by the ego that the original threats of punishment through loss of love would not be forthcoming were it not for the instinctual impulses that were felt by the child and which sought for expression. "Thus such instinctual impulses are determinants of external dangers and so become dangerous in themselves."[8] Even the desire to act sexually

[6] *Ibid.*
[7] *Ibid.*, XX, p. 139.
[8] *Ibid.*, p. 145.

121

or aggressively brings the ego's perception of loss of the object-cathexis or punishment by father. In adults, as well as in children, to some degree certain situations cause the ego to react as if the old danger situations still existed, and it responds with anxiety.[9]

Freud identified guilt and anxiety, saying that economically the threat of punishment by the super-ego, the introjected father, is perceived by the ego in the same manner as it perceives other threats to its existence, centering about experiences of separation from the loved object, to which threat the ego responds with the signal of anxiety.

Criticisms which have already been made in chapter 3 concerning Freud's theories are relevant in regard to his explication of the origin and dynamics of guilt. He was not free to pursue the implications of his observations of interpersonal relationships between mother and child and father and child because of the restrictions imposed by his presupposition of the nature of each person as a closed energy system and the internal instinctual origin of all motivation. While Freud apparently meant castration in a literal sense when he spoke of castration fear, the way in which the term is used could, it seems, be directly transliterated into the word punishment without doing violence to his genuine insights concerning the child's introjection of the perceived threatening aspects of parental behavior. It is clear that guilt in his theory is the fear of separation from a significant other person, its prototype experience being the early experiences of the fear of losing the love of the parents.

Paul Tillich

A contemporary writer who speaks of guilt in terms of anxiety is Paul Tillich. Man's being is both given to him and

[9] *Ibid.*, p. 147.

demanded of him. He is not responsible for having caused himself to exist, but once existing, in his freedom he is responsible for what he makes of himself and for the judging of the product. This is the situation out of which the anxiety of guilt arises. As a person makes his decisions, he is in the process of moral self-affirmation. But he has the power, and actually exercises it, to act in contradiction to his self-affirmation and the fulfillment of his destiny. When the person becomes aware of the ambiguity of his own actions, it is subjectively experienced as guilt, and it is present every moment [10] The realization of one's own acts towards self-negation drives one toward self-rejection, "the despair of having lost our destiny." [11] This guilt is one of the three major forms of anxiety in which nonbeing threatens being, by threatening man's moral self-affirmation, relatively in terms of guilt and absolutely in terms of condemnation.[12]

As an existential statement of the experiences and situation of man, Tillich is penetratingly descriptive. However, from the point of view of psychology his description must be judged as an inadequate model on the basis of its neglect of some theory of learning, a failure to understand the development of anxiety within an interpersonal matrix and to elaborate the implications of this and its omission of a discussion of the intrapsychic dynamics of the affect. Even some of the terminology itself, although apparently meaningful in presenting philosophical categories, does not have precise meaning in psychology.

However, both Freud and Tillich (and numerous others)

[10] *The Courage to Be* (New Haven: Yale University Press, 1952), pp. 51-52.
[11] *Ibid.*, p. 53.
[12] *Ibid.*, p. 41.

identify guilt as being anxiety, and they agree as to its universal presence in human experience. Freud clearly sees it as separation fear, and Tillich perceives it as being involved in alienation.

Experimental Evidence

To what extent is the identification of guilt and anxiety a valid viewpoint? Can it be upheld empirically? Can the process be described in terms which are not bound to the physiological instinctual conceptuality or to the philosophical terminology of existentialism which does not lend itself readily to psychological investigation?

Lowe has observed that there have been theoretical discussions linking guilt and anxiety but that there have been few empirical studies. The question arose for him when in the course of an investigation a correlation of .94 was obtained between the Psychasthenia (Pt) scale on the Minnesota Multiphasic Personality Inventory and a measure of subjective guilt feelings which he had devised. He felt that this result cast some doubt on the ability to distinguish between feelings of guilt and the anxiety reflected by the Pt scale. To study this relationship further, he administered a newly devised measure of guilt and a validated anxiety scale to three groups of subjects. The statistically significant correlations between the scales led Lowe to the conclusion that what has been referred to as guilt and as anxiety are in fact the same affect. The two are equivalent, and any distinction between them is to be understood primarily as a variance in terminology.[13]

[13] C. Marshall Lowe, "The Equivalence of Guilt and Anxiety as Psychological Constructs," *Journal of Consulting Psychology*, XXVIII (1964), 554.

Guilt, Hostility, and Grief

The Interpersonal Approach

The central value of one's life is seen as being in relation to another. The super-ego, or conscience, or whatever term might be appropriately chosen to refer to the introjected rewarding and punishing behavior of the parents, clearly takes form in the context of the child's seeking to gain and maintain the love and approval of those upon whom he has learned to be dependent as a self. Although learning theory has many complexities about it, it remains generally true that behavior which is rewarded (need fulfilled, tension reduced) tends to be stamped in and behavior which is punished (directly through pain in some form or which is not rewarded or gratified and thus allows for increase of tension) tends to be extinguished. The first perceptions of the rewarding and punishing behavior of the parents are linked with their basic physiological need-fulfilling behavior toward the infant. As time passes, and with the maintenance of the dependency relationship, their approval and disapproval is interpreted as reward and punishment. Behavior which signals their approval is learned. It is also learned that other behavior signals their disapproval. This behavior is perceived to be threatening to the relationship and thereby threatening to one's self, which cannot be first understood as secure and separate apart from the parent. McKenzie put it: "the need for *security and safety* is awakened at the same time it is jeopardized." [14] The need and the threat are learned conjointly. The perception of this danger of separation is what was defined in the last chapter as anxiety, and which here is called guilt simply because that which threatens the relationship is one's own behavior, or his failure to behave in a certain way, or even his thinking or feeling forbidden, dis-

[14] John G. McKenzie, *Guilt: Its Meaning and Significance* (Nashville: Abingdon Press, 1962), p. 31.

approved behavior. Therefore, "the anxiety of guilt is just this anxiety of being loved no longer." [15] The identifications with the parents, i.e., the learning of approved and disapproved behavior along with the strong affect created by the situation of intense need, comprise the original foundation upon which the anxiety of guilt is built.

Tournier emphasizes the inter- as well as the intrapersonal nature of guilt-anxiety. Recognizing the validity of Tillich's approach, he speaks of the refusal to develop one's full selfhood or to assume one's proper responsibility in a situation as issuing in the "guilt of self toward self," and the actual violation of human relationships as a "guilt toward others." [16] Yet even in this "true" guilt, that not of a neurotic nature, there is always a residue of the infantile origin of guilt-anxiety, always "a little of the fear of losing the love and esteem of others which constituted infantile guilt," [17] or anxiety.

It should be clear that these are not guilt-anxiety feelings which arise for the first time out of the Oedipal situation or, if one does not accept the literal Freudian statement of it, out of whatever personal interaction there is between father-mother and child at this stage of the child's life. Rather, guilt-anxiety begins to take form with the first experiences of the child as they were described in chapter 4. It was stated that the first internalization is that of the mother, as she as the external ego becomes the core of the internal ego. Not only is her accepting and need-fulfilling behavior internalized as a part of the infant's primitive perception of himself, but so also is her punishing and disapproving behavior, including her leaving, the experience of her absence. This is the primitive super-ego. Thus the psychic force which produces the subjective experi-

[15] Paul Tournier, *Guilt and Grace* (New York: Harper, 1962), p. 189.
[16] *Ibid.*, p. 65.
[17] *Ibid.*, p. 91.

ence of guilt is the introjected leaving (punishing, rejecting)-needed mother and the punishing-needed father, precisely the terms in which anxiety was described as developing in the previous chapter. Guilt is anxiety, fear of separation from those upon whom one depends for his selfhood.

HOSTILITY, AMBIVALENCE, AND GUILT

Not only has guilt been spoken of as being frequently (or universally, depending upon the writer) observed as involved in grief, but so also has hostility. Rarely is this hostility directed overtly toward the deceased. It is usually either turned inward upon the grief sufferer himself or toward others related to the situation. Occasionally this hostility may, as Zilboorg has suggested, be a defensive measure to counteract the fear felt, and without any real object to direct it against, the bereaved expresses it toward any available person.[18] Even more pertinent, however, is the fact that some degree of hostility has always been involved in the relationship with the deceased and that in more than one way this in itself is productive of guilt-anxiety.

The first part of the task is to show the origin of ambivalence as a universal human experience, and the second is to demonstrate that hostility is productive of guilt-anxiety.

The Universality of Ambivalence

If there were a mother who was perfectly loving, without any anxiety at all herself, who consistently met every need of the infant and small child, and who never frustrated the self-expressions of the developing self, it might be assumed that this mother's child might not develop elements of hatred,

---

[18] Gregory Zilboorg, "Fear of Death," *Psychoanalytic Quarterly*, XII (1943), 473-74.

hostility, and aggression in the relationship. To the degree that the mother is *not* this, to that degree will there be such negative emotions mixed with the positive responses. Macmurray assumes the absolute need of the child for the mother as this need has been elaborated in chapter 3 and therefore the strong motivation of the child to do whatever she requires, even though it be perceived in opposition to his own developing selfhood.[19] If the mother's behavior is not need fulfilling, then there is the learned perception of threat to the self. The experience is the same as "Mother does not love me," or even, "Mother is against me." The response to this is, "Then I am against her," aggression.[20] It should be noted that this feeling of aggression toward the mother does not always issue in direct aggressive behavior, but might be dealt with by any one of a number of mechanisms. Yet it is there and a part of the relationship. The mother's task is to enable the child to see his judgment as an illusion. To the degree that she cannot, and falls short of perfection as stated above, the judgment is not an illusion. Therefore, the child's first and most important relationship is always established upon mixed motivation, ambivalent feelings. It always contains the element of the fear of withdrawal of support and the aggression against the frustrating mother, mixed with the positive affect of trust and love.[21] There is then "fear for oneself in relation to the Other, and the defence of oneself against the threat from the Other." [22]

Ambivalence, including hostility and aggression, is inevitably a motivating force in every meaningful relationship, growing out of the original most significant relation with the

[19] Macmurray, *Persons in Relation*, pp. 98-99.
[20] *Ibid.*, p. 100.
[21] *Ibid.*, pp. 101-3.
[22] *Ibid.*, p. 104.

mother and the inability of any person to fulfill consistently all of the pressing needs of another, arousing fear of loss of support and a tendency toward aggression. It now needs to be shown that this aggression itself, rising out of the fear of separation, further threatens the relationship, creating guilt-anxiety.

The Relationship of Hostility to Guilt

It must be remembered that the real danger is the loss of meaningful relationship with another person, a relationship which one has learned is necessary for his own selfhood, the integrity, wholeness, and life of one's self. The separation from another with whom one has been emotionally linked, where some degree of identification has taken place, is perceived as self loss, the disintegration of one's self. The response to this is anxiety.

An internal drive, whatever it may be, is not inherently, in and of itself, to be feared. At the same time, Freud has already been quoted as showing how the expression of instinctual impulses would be a determinant of an external danger to the ego, and therefore these impulses come to be felt as dangerous in themselves. Horney has picked up this insight, but has moved away from the instinctual bias and the exclusively sexual emphasis and terminology to what would seem to be a more appropriate conceptuality for an understanding of grief and other areas of human experience. Recognizing that there are psychic conditions which can create a feeling of danger to a person and at the same time an attitude of helplessness toward it, Horney indicates that any impulse has the potential power to stimulate anxiety if its discovery or expression would conflict with other vital interests or needs.[23] The position

[23] Horney, *The Neurotic Personality of Our Time* (New York: W. W. Norton, 1937), pp. 61-62.

already made clear in this book is that meaningful relations with others is a central, learned value of human life. Horney posits hostile impulses as being the most prevalent of the drives which would be perceived as a threat to this stated value, and therefore as being the main source of anxiety.[24] The very meaning of hostility and its expression implies a moving against another, inherently involving threat of separation. It should be admitted that this is not wholly unrealistic, for on the whole people in most cultures have not learned to deal constructively with overt aggression without the modification, at least temporarily, of one's perception of the relationship as being one which is stable and secure. The expression of hostility usually carries with it the reaction of breach of relations. Thus, it produces anxiety, for, as Horney has observed, "one may love or need a person at the same time that one is hostile toward him." [25] Either the perception of the hostility by the other is interpreted by the hostile person as meaning rejection by the loved and needed one, or the feelings of hostility are in conflict with the learned, idealized image of oneself and therefore felt as threatening to the self which it is necessary to be in order to have the approval of others. These are ways of expressing the same events in the developmental process. The first expressions of aggression by the infant and small child are met with disapproval and suppressive measures. The fear on the part of the child that the needed relationship is being broken is met by the repression of the feelings and the learning that one is not really a person who feels hostility.

Such repression of hostility intensifies the anxiety, because it reinforces the feeling of being defenseless against threat by robbing a person of the impulses he actually needs to cope with

[24] *Ibid.*, p. 63.
[25] *Ibid.*, p. 66.

130

threat.[26] This anxiety is what is spoken of when one uses the term guilt. One learns to "feel guilty" over the feelings and expression of hostility by the punishment, disapproval, and perceived, if not actual, withdrawal of support by the parents upon whom one has learned to be wholly dependent. This fear of loss of support, being a punishment which is temporally contiguous with the expression of hostility, is a response which is stamped in, to be cued off in the future by even the feeling of hostility, the desire for aggression. In the mind of the infant and small child, the desire is not distinguishable from the act, so the punishment received for the act is feared when the desire alone is present. This is a part of the introjection of parental attitude toward the child which is called the super-ego, from which springs the feeling called guilt, one's own judgment that hostility is to be feared because it means loss of relationship.

Hostility, which inevitably arises out of the interaction in any close, meaningful emotional relationship, thus creating ambivalent feelings, further threatens the relationship and is productive of guilt-anxiety. Guilt, then, as anxiety is inescapable as an aspect of the anxiety of grief itself.

GUILT AND GRIEF

Tournier has stated that "there is no grave beside which a flood of guilt feelings does not assail the mind." [27] His observation is merely a summary of the reports of many writers on grief. But precisely how is guilt seen as an integral part of the grief reaction?

[26] *Ibid.*, p. 64.
[27] Tournier, *Guilt and Grace*, p. 93.

The Dynamic Source of Guilt in Grief

It has been stated above that ambivalent feelings are involved in all relationships; it was further shown that the hostile feelings are productive of guilt. Therefore, there are areas of every meaningful interpersonal relationship that are colored by guilt-anxiety. When the death of an emotionally significant person occurs, guilt-anxiety is triggered in a number of ways.

Regression. First, as a reaction to the stress of the situation, the separation anxiety aroused, there is a tendency toward regression, as discussed in chapter 4. This regression takes one back emotionally to more primitive behavioral responses; one is closer to the origin of his emotional behavior, and there is the tendency to feel unworthy in one's own eyes in regard to hostile feelings subjectively experienced and/or expressed. The primitive super-ego accuses one of being responsible for breaking the relationship. In this instance, the guilt-anxiety operating is not necessarily related to the hostile impulses toward the deceased. Rather, the separation anxiety stimulated by the death activates the mechanism of regression, which allows the bereaved to feel the threat and punishment for his ambivalent feelings toward the original significant others. Out of the regressive tendencies can even arise additional feelings of hostility and anxiety as the death of the other is interpreted as desertion by him.

A man whose infancy and childhood was spent with a cold and depriving mother grew up with intense hostility toward her. Because of the inhibiting measures of the parents and the child's need to salvage whatever security he could in his situation of dependency, these hostile feelings were repressed. As a young man he married a woman who met his needs quite adequately, and while his repressed hostility was the source of some times of tension, a meaningful relationship was established during the years of marriage. However, upon her death, this drastic separation from one upon whom he was so dependent emotionally triggered intense anxiety, and along with it a regression to the earlier stages in which anxiety was mixed with a great hostility. These feelings now broke out in aggressive attitudes and words and resistive behavior toward those around him, interspersed with periods of considerable guilt. Neither the hostility expressed nor the guilt felt were in their intensity related directly to his wife, but were regressive to his earlier feelings toward his mother.

Identification of wish and act. Second, it was related above that the unconscious does not perceive the difference between wish and act. This situation has come about because of the preverbal and even preconceptual learning of the arousal of fear of separation as a result of having aggressive feelings, because parental disapproval of aggressive behavior is expressed toward the infant and small child. Thus the residue of parataxic reasoning allows one to feel that his hostile wishes against the other have somehow been causally related to the separation, later the death. Again, one feels responsible for the act which has broken the relationship, so there is guilt-anxiety. But since this feeling of responsibility is painful, it is dealt with by repression or some other mechanism. It should be emphasized that there is no "real" or "true" guilt at this point, only guilt feelings rising out of early learned patterns of responding.

Violation of relationship. However, such real guilt should not be overlooked as an important factor in much grief. This is the third manner in which guilt-anxiety is constitutive of grief. Certainly in most relationships there have been elements of the violation of the other which Tournier referred to as a value guilt, "a guilt toward others," having its source in our failure as persons in our responsibility toward them, a person's "consciousness of having betrayed an authentic standard." [28]

At this point there should be some modification of the earlier statement that irrational guilt feelings arise out of the early learning to intensify the anxiety of grief, and that in these feelings there is no true guilt, true guilt presupposing responsibility. The acceptance of the fact that hostile feelings are universal does not mean that an individual is entirely blameless in regard to the intensity of those feelings and the degree to which they are actually productive of alienation within the relationship. To the degree that aggressive feelings are nourished and cultivated and used to destroy the other as a person, there is true guilt, the responsibility for violating the other. Anyone who has been involved in a large number of grief situations has heard the bereaved searching back through the history of the relationship and recounting words and acts that wronged the other and the failures to minister adequately to the needs of the other. Although this process is obviously intensified, occasionally even to the degree of morbidity, by unconscious factors already mentioned, the influence of genuine guilt itself should not be minimized. Things do go wrong in a relationship; guilt-anxiety is felt, and appropriately so.

It would seem that real guilt is intensified and brought to awareness with greater force at the time of the death of the other because the death cuts off opportunities for atonement, forgiveness, reconciliation. The bereaved finds his need for forgiveness, the healing of the broken aspects of the relationship, frustrated, and he is faced with the prospect of having to

[28] *Ibid.,* pp. 64-65.

134

Guilt, Hostility, and Grief

live with his guilt. There seems to be no way of working through the ambivalent feelings.

Mowrer has spoken of the reality of the attitudes and behavior which violate the learned social strictures that are necessary for harmonious living with one another. Guilt is the learned fear of punishment which comes with the violation of the standards. Flight from the guilt is ordinarily impossible, although it can be repressed, thereby producing even greater anxiety. Therefore, the healthier way of dealing with the situation of guilt is to accept its punishment and use it as a stimulus to become more responsible and more mature.[29]

Inability to perform social role. Another possible source of guilt at the time of the death of a person very close to one is referred to by Volkart. There is a social expectation of a particular role that the bereaved should play. Yet the ambivalent feelings of the bereaved may prevent his completely performing this role. His social fear may be so strong that his failure to do so may be felt as guilt-anxiety.[30] For example, not everyone cries as readily or as vigorously as everyone else. Yet there are many places in which the expectation concerning mourning is that it be overtly demonstrative. The reticent individual on the one hand is not able to produce the required amount of tears and recognizes that this is the way he really is, yet the social expectation and his need of social approval may both be so strong that he may wonder about the validity of his response and feel guilty because of what is perceived as his emotional inadequacy.

Or if there is the custom in certain locations of the use of elaborate caskets and expensive headstones, the person who

[29] Mowrer, "Pain, Punishment and Anxiety," *Anxiety*, ed. Paul Hoch and Joseph Zubin (New York: Grune & Stratton, 1950), p. 36.
[30] Volkart and Michael, "Bereavement and Mental Health," pp. 297-98.

is unable or unwilling to pay these amounts may be made to feel that he has not loved the deceased sufficiently and feelings of guilt result.

The Expressions of Guilt in Grief

These are some of the ways in which the anxiety of guilt is involved as an integral part of the grief-anxiety reaction. How does this guilt express itself; how is it observed and reported?

Subjective experience. First, one must not ignore the obvious. People often consciously feel the guilt and they themselves report it. There are self-recriminations for real or supposed wrongs done to the deceased and expressions of failure to be responsible to the person. This is all conscious, though it is not to deny unconscious dynamics at work. In fact, the grief-stricken person may even be aware of the irrational nature of the strength of the feelings, yet they are clearly present and identifiable by him.

Hostility. A second way in which guilt-anxiety is seen operating in the bereaved is through the expression of hostility. It has been shown that ambivalent emotions are in all close relationships and that hostility is productive of guilt. To be sure, in many instances this is not a major complicating factor. Nevertheless, when hostility in any of its forms is exhibited noticeably in the bereaved, the anxiety of guilt is involved. As was stated earlier, this hostility is seldom directed toward the deceased; most of the time this would not be compatible with one's self-image or society's expectation of the mourner's role and would be too anxiety producing. Therefore, the aggressive behavior is either displaced onto other persons within the situation or turned inward upon oneself.

Guilt, Hostility, and Grief

Behavior ranging from irritability in general to overt aggression toward specific other persons is a relatively common observation in bereavement.[31] This is frequently linked with a hypomanic response on the part of the bereaved, and points to an underlying anger or hostility. Becker has listed a category of bereavement reaction as excited, and notes that aggressive behavior and an underlying anger is present.[32] Irritability, aggression, and outbursts of temper are a part of the clinical picture of hypomania, which is listed as a subclassification of the affective disorders. This behavior can be understood in two ways. First, as Stern suggests, it is the projection of the hated aspects of the dead person onto available living persons.[33] Since the object is gone, there is displacement of hostility. Second, the self-accusations of guilt-anxiety over the hostile feelings are intolerable, so the feelings of self-loathing are projected outward onto others. Either way, it is a hostility-guilt-anxiety crisis with which the individual is seeking to deal and against which he must defend his self-structure. Any mania is probably a mechanism to ward off the intolerable feelings of worthlessness, guilt, self-blame, which are a part of depression, and it is not uncommon for a depression to follow closely a manic phase of behavior.[34]

A more common response to the dynamics of hostility-guilt in grief is to turn the aggression inward upon oneself as depression. Fulcomer found elements of depression in many of the responses of grief in the immediate, postimmediate, and transitional stages, with responses of self-blame, despair, de-

---

[31] Bowlby, "Grief and Mourning in Infancy and Early Childhood," p. 17; Lindemann, "Symptomatology," p. 14; Stern, "Grief Reactions in Later Life," p. 289.

[32] Howard Becker, "The Sorrow of Bereavement," *Journal of Abnormal and Social Psychology*, XXVII (1933), 395.

[33] Stern, "Grief Reactions in Later Life," p. 293.

[34] Coleman, *Abnormal Psychology and Modern Life*, p. 335.

jection, nonactivity, inattention to external stimuli, self-absorption, detachment, feelings of exhaustion, occasionally with weeping, but frequently with little or no weeping.[35] These are among the symptoms of the clinical picture of depression. It is well accepted that there is in the background of this response a severe childhood discipline, a punitive super-ego, especially in the area of the prevention of the overt expression of hostility. Especially pertinent to the situation of grief is the element of hostility toward former love-objects.[36]

Apparently his (the depressive's) rigid conscience leads to an intropunitive reaction to his life difficulties, and the hostility aroused by his frustrations and failures is turned inward toward the self rather than being directed toward the outside world.[37]

This, of course, is not a new idea. Abraham referred to the hostility involved in all depression, and in the case of grief, interpreted the response as a result of the bereaved person's seeking to maintain the lost love-object by introjection. However, to the degree that introjection is successful and to the degree that there is hostility, it is clear that the unconscious hostility toward the object is experienced as hostility toward one's self.[38]

The deeper the depressive reaction is in bereavement, the more one would suspect a strong ambivalent conflict and a high degree of guilt.[39] The behavioral responses of depression are attempts to cope with the separation anxiety cued off by the loss of a cathected object.

It should be emphasized that the depressive response is not

[35] Fulcomer, "The Adjustive Behavior," pp. 96, 110, 119, 127.
[36] Coleman, *Abnormal Psychology and Modern Life,* pp. 334, 336-37.
[37] *Ibid.,* p. 336.
[38] Abraham, *Selected Papers,* p. 435.
[39] Deutsch, "Absence of Grief," p. 13.

in direct proportion simply to the amount of hostility felt, but to the intensity of the conflict of ambivalent feelings: the degree of hostility set over against the degree to which one has learned that hostility is a threat to relationship, threatening separation from one who is also loved and needed.

A clear illustration of the relationship of the dynamics of hostility and guilt as they relate to grief was presented by a female college student who, after a suicide attempt, was referred to a counselor. She was so deeply depressed that at first communication was quite difficult. Gradually a picture was pieced together. The first part of it was the information that her father had died about a year and a half before and that there had been a suicide attempt on her part within a few months after that event. In discussing the father's death, the information was divulged that her father and mother were divorced. The father had remarried, but the student had lived with her mother who had not remarried. She frequently visited her father and kept a close relationship with him. During one long, intensely emotional silence, in response to the question, "What are you feeling now?", the student replied, "I want to destroy something." What did she want to destroy? First, herself; then, anything; finally, her mother.

She had developed an unusually strong attachment to her father. At the time her parents were divorced when she was about eight, she held her mother responsible for it, and had tremendous hostility toward her which could be only partially expressed because of her dependence on the mother. When the father died this whole psychic conflict was reactivated, with the new force of several years of repressed hostility. There even seemed to be the unconscious accusation that the mother was responsible for the father's death.

In a sense she had mourned for her father, yet the mourning was also incomplete in that she had not worked out the unusu-

139

ally close feelings to him and the hostility toward the mother, whom she needed, loved, and hated. For these feelings of hatred she felt guilty (feared separation from her), and these were an intensifying and complicating factor in the grief, in that they were not openly expressed in some satisfactory fashion, but were turned inward upon the self.

Even though this situation differed from many of those discussed, since the basic hostility was not toward the deceased, it does show the relation of hostility and guilt as additive to the anxiety of grief, and how it expresses itself in bereavement as depression.

Self-punishing behavior. Hostility-guilt-anxiety also expresses itself and can be observed in grief in the self-punishing behavior of the bereaved. Much of this is related to depression: mental suffering, self-blame, the refusal to eat, the rejection of the help of others, withdrawal from society. Guilt-anxiety by its nature, its development within the context of the punishing-threatening behavior of the parents, asks for punishment. Punishment has early been learned to be sought when there was behavior by the child which threatened separation, because punishment itself was rewarding. It brought the physical presence of the parent and the restoration of the relationship. Therefore, when guilt-anxiety is experienced in grief, it is not difficult to understand that varying degrees of self-punishing behavior should be sought. One form of this is depression, aggression turned inward.

All self-punishing elements are not to be subsumed under depressive reaction, however. Excessive activity which punishes one's body is one form. It has even been suggested that somatic illnesses following grief may play this role. Stern has found that illness not infrequently follows bereavement, especially among older people who make fewer overt expressions of guilt than those younger. The question is raised whether the self-punishment of the illness might be a substitute act for the otherwise unexpressed guilt.[40]

Self-justifying behavior. A final clue to the possible operation of guilt-anxiety as a dynamic force in a grief reaction is the observation of compensatory and self-justifying behavior. Where there is excessive display of emotions or exaggerated idealization of the deceased or the relationship with the deceased or if the mourning behavior continues over a much longer period of time than usual, then an intense ambivalent conflict and the operation of guilt-anxiety might be suspected.

Fulcomer entitles one of the observed categories of behavior in the transitional stage of mourning as "Attention-Getting." Under this title are listed an emphasis on overt mourning, the desire to tell one's troubles over and over again to any listener, frequent weeping, rejecting and resenting help from others, and the overemphasizing of affectional attachments.[41] Although any one or more of these items of behavior may frequently enter into the behavior of bereavement at least to some degree, all of them to a great degree are excessive, and one might suspect that hostility-guilt-anxiety is greater than usual.

Illustrative of the self-justifying behavior are the reactions of a husband at the time of the death and funeral of his wife. She had been ill for several years, with their both knowing of the terminal nature of the disease. During the last two years she had had several major, extensive surgeries, and had been

---

[40] Stern, *"Grief Reactions in Later Life,"* p. 292.
[41] Fulcomer, *"The Adjustive Behavior,"* p. 135.

almost completely confined to wheel chair and bed the last twelve months. There had been time and opportunity for some preliminary mourning by the husband to take place, especially since the wife had been quite willing to discuss her impending death and plans for the funeral and even the life of the family after her death.

Prior to the funeral, the husband was not far from collapse and there were frequent periods of deep weeping. When he did talk, he went into great detail concerning the deceased's perfection as a wife and mother, the large amounts of money he had spent for medical care, the fact that the best doctors of the state had been treating her, how he had spared no time or expense. There was continual seeking for support of the fact that he had done everything he could. Although the burial was in a very modest cemetery, with people of only modest means present, an extremely costly vault and casket combination and headstone were used.

Aspects of mourning before the fact had taken place. But as the wife lived on this mourning process not only reached the point of diminishing returns, it was reversed, as feelings of hostility began to be felt by the husband toward the wife who did not die when she was supposed to, and who lived on to disrupt the family situation. This hostility and the intense guilt felt over it were the motivating forces behind the excessive nature of the expressions of grief, the self-justifying and compensatory behavior.

SUMMARY

Grief involves separation anxiety as its major dynamic element. Guilt, too, has been considered to be a form of anxiety.

When its form is carefully examined in respect to its dynamic origins in relationship to mother-father, it, too, is seen to be separation anxiety, the perception of a threat to the self arising from separation from a significant other. The approval-disapproval of meaningful others has been introjected as a vital part of one's own self. Guilt, when it is spoken of in relation to grief, is not a separate and distinguishable affect, but is part and parcel of the anxiety of grief.

The second major consideration is that the anxiety which is called guilt is always present in grief and it is only a matter of the degree to which it operates to increase the intensity of the reaction. Ambivalent feelings are always involved in significant relationships. This is both the primitive learned response to the first relationship and the actual fact within every succeeding close relationship. Hostile, aggressive feelings inevitably arise out of the mother's inability to meet every need on the part of the infant as soon as it appears. The infant's frustration cues aggression. But aggression is met with disapproval and the fear of the loss of the other is learned to be connected with these feelings. In this context, the anxiety is called guilt, and it is the result of the feeling and expressions of hostility. In later relationships, needs are not totally met either. There is frustration, aggression, feelings of guilt, fear of loss of the other.

Guilt-anxiety operates in the grief situation through the mechanism of regression, which allows for a reexpression of early ambivalent feelings and their corresponding guilt-anxiety, through the unconscious feeling that the hostile wishes directed against the deceased have caused his death and that one is responsible for the separation, through genuine violations of the other as a person which tend to destroy relationship, and through the introjected fear of society as a result of not fulfilling social expectation in the role of the bereaved.

This guilt-anxiety expresses itself and can be observed in grief: first, as a conscious and articulated subjective experience; second, as hostility toward others and hostility turned inward and experienced and observed as depression; in self-punishing, and finally, in self-justifying and compensatory behavior.

6
Existential Anxiety in Grief

The fact that people fear their own death is not a new commentary on human life. Yet the verbal formulations of this idea and its relationship to the lives of persons vary drastically. In the midst of a culture which on the whole seeks to avoid the personal issue of death, an emphasis on the role in one's motivational life of the fear of death comes from two main sources: psychoanalysis and existentialism. Although these two approaches are couched in different terms, they reinforce one another in regard to the reality of anxiety about one's own death.

This chapter will seek to present the emphasis of existentialism concerning the dynamic force in human life of the idea of one's finitude, the source of existential anxiety. It will be seen that investigators in other fields have also noticed the prevalence of fear of death and man's need for meaning, and that a number of them feel that the death of a person with whom an individual has been closely involved emotionally acts as a strong stimulus in the arousal of one's own fears concerning the fact that he, too, will die. This anxiety is an element in the grief reaction. However, an attempt will be made to demonstrate that what has been called existential anxiety has in its dynamic origins the same separation anxiety that has already been elaborated in chapter 4 as a universal human experience and which is the dominant affect in grief.

EXISTENTIALISTIC PHILOSOPHERS AND THEOLOGIANS

Sören Kierkegaard

The groundwork for contemporary existentialism was laid by Sören Kierkegaard. The starting point is the givenness of the individual's existence, the nothingness which is defined in terms of possibility, radical freedom out of which comes anxiety-guilt-sin. The nothingness in man is the lack which leads to free choice, free act. The awareness of possibility and total responsibility produces dread (*Angst*, anxiety). This dread is similar to fear, but is different from it in that fear has reference to a specific object whereas dread does not.

Kierkegaard has used the biblical myth of Adam to describe the dynamics of anxiety-guilt and its origin. It was God's prohibition which awakened "in him the possibility of freedom,

. . . the alarming possibility of being able." [1] But Adam (every-man) does not know specifically *what* he is able to do or become. This is the source of ambivalent feelings toward the unknown object of his dread: he loves it, is attracted toward it, yet he fears it and flees from it. The subjective experience is that of guilt, the loving of that which one fears.[2] "Dread is the dizziness of freedom, (when) freedom . . . gazes down into its own possibility, grasping at finiteness to sustain itself. In this dizziness, freedom succumbs." [3]

The source of anxiety, then, is in reality within one's self, not in any given external situation. There is no real external object to be feared; there is rather nothing, no-thing. However, there is always the tendency for anxiety to seek an object, some *thing* rather than no-thing, for in this way the painful feelings may be more readily controlled. "The nothing which is the object of dread becomes . . . more and more a something." [4] The answer to anxiety, though, is not to be found in evasion, or in any thing, but in acknowledgment of the anxiety for what it is, acceptance of it as a part of one's self, and allowing it to carry one to faith.[5]

Martin Heidegger

All twentieth-century existentialist writers are greatly dependent upon Kierkegaard's basic concepts and emphases, however differently they may develop their thought. One of the more influential of these is Martin Heidegger.

Heidegger's fundamental presupposition in his analysis of

---

[1] *Concept of Dread* (Princeton: Princeton University Press, 1944), p. 40.

[2] *Ibid.*, p. 39.

[3] *Ibid.*, p. 55.

[4] *Ibid.*

[5] *Ibid.*, pp. 142-45.

being is the priority of the questions which each individual being asks about his *own* being. The question is not primarily about "being-in-general," but about the personal existing being.[6] The only way any person can begin to think of being is through his own being, his own living of the life that is now his. To be existing also means to have possibility, potentiality to be fully oneself.[7] This being who exists, the person, is in his existence one who fears. That about which he fears is his own existence, fear for one's self.

Even if the fear seems to be for something or someone else, the essential nature of fear as being for one's self is not changed. That with which one identifies his own being *is* a part of his existence, and when this other is threatened, he himself is threatened, and the response is fear for one's own being. Heidgger makes this explicit when he discusses "fearing for the Other" as "being-afraid-for-*oneself*," for "what one 'is apprehensive about' is one's Being-with the Other, who might be torn away." [8]

Since a person is "thrown-into-the-world" and left alone with freedom and the potentiality for Being, he may exercise this freedom in the direction either of authentic or inauthentic existence. The former is "the Self which has been taken hold of in its own way," as contrasted with the "they-self," the person who is directed so by others that he never realizes his own uniqueness and potential.[9] To choose the latter route is the *"fleeing* of Dasein (the existing person) in the face of itself," giving up the possibility of authenticity, and is related to the topic of anxiety.[10] Anxiety is not the fear of entities in

[6] *Being and Time* (New York: Harper, 1962), p. 33.
[7] *Ibid.*, p. 183.
[8] *Ibid.*, p. 181.
[9] *Ibid.*, p. 167.
[10] *Ibid.*, p. 229.

the world; rather anxiety makes one turn *to* things in the world and absorb oneself in them. One is anxious simply concerning his own "Being-in-the-world" as such.[11] There is no definite object which is the source of the anxiety. One cannot perceive or locate the source. To exist is to have anxiety. Yet things in the world do not offer relief from it, and so anxiety pushes a person to the realization that he cannot understand himself in terms of the world. Therefore, it throws him "back upon that which he is anxious about—(his) authentic potentiality-for-Being-in-the-world." [12] Man is revealed to himself by the force of anxiety as being free to choose himself, to affirm himself, to take responsibility for himself, and to the degree that he does so, he chooses authenticity.

Integrally related to the concept of anxiety as a given of Being-in-the-world is the awareness of death as a limitation of Being. This awareness of death is self-evidently perceived as a threat to Being, and in the face of it persons react with anxiety. The meaning of dying is to be "no-longer-in-the-world." This cannot be fully encountered in one's own death, but can be viewed in the death of another. Yet there is a phenomenal element of content missing, since what is left is merely a material Thing.

In one literal sense, the dead person is no longer present. In another sense, however, and one just as phenomenologically real, there is a Being-with the deceased just as a person can always be-with another. But those left behind still *cannot* experience with the deceased his "Being-come-to-an-end." They are only "there-alongside"; the dying of the Other is not experienced.[13] In other words, the meaning of having died obviously is a question which cannot be answered by the person who

[11] *Ibid.*, p. 230.
[12] *Ibid.*, p. 232.
[13] *Ibid.*, p. 282.

has in fact experienced it. A person can only analyze his own Being-toward the death of another.

To summarize the discussion of death to this point: there belongs to the existing person so long as he exists a not-yet which will inevitably come to pass. This not-yet is the non-existence of this present Being, and is a form of experience which can only be unique for one's own self; no one else can undergo it for us.[14]

If, then, an essential part of the existing person is in reality not-yet, then he must become, or even *be,* what is not-yet. The moving toward what is not-yet is a characteristic of Being. In this sense, "Death is a way to be, which Dasein takes over as soon as it is." [15]

Within this conceptual scheme, the term "dying" does not refer to that one event at which time life physiologically ends, but to the whole way of Being of a person, and to analyze dying is a way of understanding life itself.[16] It is a necessary task, then, to interpret "death as Being-towards the end." [17] Being must be oriented toward its possibility, its not-yet. Death stands before all persons; therefore, life must be lived in the knowledge that death is not to be escaped. Yet in his Being as given, a person does not have clear and experiential knowledge that death is a part of his Being. This condition of existence presents itself to him primarily in that state of mind which has been termed anxiety. Anxiety is always anxiety in the face of death, for this is an inescapable part of Being-in-the-world. That which is feared is one's own potentiality-for-Being. This anxiety in the face of death is not the same response as fear of one's demise, but as a fundamental condition

[14] *Ibid.,* p. 286.
[15] *Ibid.,* p. 289.
[16] *Ibid.,* p. 291.
[17] *Ibid.,* p. 293.

of existence it is disclosed to a person that he exists only as one who is existing toward his end.

Usually as a person lives, he flees from, covers up, this aspect of his Being. This means that one's behavioral responses which result from such fleeing and covering up are the overt symptoms of an inauthentic existence. One way in which this is exhibited is by the acceptance of a public interpretation of death which depersonalizes it, which sees it as an event apart from one's own Being. It is not yet present "for me" and is not a threat. This view robs one of the opportunity for having courage to experience anxiety in the face of death. Even before a person's coming into being, society has determined his state of mind toward death. The anxiety of facing one's own whole Being has been transformed into an ambiguous fear concerning a coming event. One can usually evade this fear, so the total result is the alienation of a person from his own potentiality-for-being. Rather than being removed as an everyday issue, however, the not-yet of one's Being is constantly a motivating force.[18]

The intellectual certainty which all people have about their own death is not normally emotionally integrated into a mode of living. It is not an authentic certainty. It is not a doubting of the fact, but is an inappropriate manner of holding truth in one's Being, primarily because one defers the matter to a later time and an impersonal mode. That which is overlooked is the personalness of death and its possibility for the individual *at any moment.* Overlooking this, the character of death is veiled. The existential conception of death is that it is always a part of the Being of a person who is by virtue of his being moving toward his end. But he does not inevitably have to

[18] *Ibid.,* pp. 295-99.

evade this not-yet which is a part of his Being. He can understand his own possibility in an authentic manner.[19]

First, the actuality of one's death must be *expected* by him. But its actuality would rob him of his Being-in-the-world. Thus a person is set free in his anticipation and can understand himself in his own potentiality-for-Being. This is done primarily by being torn away from bondage to social conformity. It forces the individual *alone* to assume responsibility for himself, since he understands that death is not a general category but that it lays its claim upon an individual, himself. Anticipation does not allow a person to feel that death can be avoided, thereby freeing him to choose those possibilities for his life which would be eliminated if he were bound to evasive tactics. He is free to accept his whole Being and all of his possibilities. The certainty of death is not computed by the number of cases of death encountered, but by opening oneself to the constant threat which is given in Being.[20] In this opening of himself a person faces the "nothing" of his own possible nonexistence. He is anxious *about* his "potentiality-for-Being," which includes his death. Therefore, "Being-toward-death is essentially anxiety." [21]

Heidegger makes a summary statement of authentic Being-toward-death:

Anticipation reveals to Dasein its lostness in the they-self, and brings it face to face with the possibility of being itself, primarily unsupported by concernful solicitude, but of being itself, rather, in an impassioned *freedom towards death*—a freedom which has been released from the illusions of the "they," and which is factical, certain of itself, and anxious.[22]

[19] *Ibid.*, pp. 299-304.
[20] *Ibid.*, pp. 304-10.
[21] *Ibid.*, p. 310.
[22] *Ibid.*, p. 311.

Existential Anxiety in Grief

Paul Tillich

Tillich roots his analysis of anxiety in his concept of man as finite freedom. Man is the animal who can ask the ontological question, "Why is there being? Why is there not rather nothing?" He can look beyond the limits of his own being, but in so doing is forced to the recognition of his limits. He is forced to consider the question of nonbeing, his own being nothing. The very structure which makes negative judgment possible demonstrates that nonbeing, negation, is a part of the structure of being itself.[23]

The concrete form of nonbeing which makes this type of expression personally powerful for a person is death.

The anticipation of nothingness at death gives human existence its existential character. Sartre includes in nonbeing not only the threat of nothingness but also the threat of meaninglessness (i.e., the destruction of the structure of being).[24]

For man the real problem of nonbeing is the problem of finitude. Finitude is being limited by nonbeing, the "not yet" and "no more" of being. To be, therefore, is to be finite.[25] But this does not fully define man. He belongs to more than finitude because he has the power of infinite self-transcendence, "an expression of (his) belonging to that which is beyond nonbeing, to being-itself." [26] It is out of man's understanding of himself in this way that anxiety arises.

Finitude in awareness is anxiety. . . . It cannot be derived; it can only be seen and described. . . . Anxiety is independent of any

[23] *Systematic Theology* (Chicago: University of Chicago Press, 1951), I, 186-87.
[24] *Ibid.*, p. 189.
[25] *Ibid.*, pp. 189-90.
[26] *Ibid.*, p. 191.

The Dynamics of Grief

special object which might produce it; it is dependent only on the threat of nonbeing. . . . In this sense it has been rightly said that the object of anxiety is nothingness.[27]

It is not clear to this reader of Tillich just exactly what he means when he says that anxiety "cannot be derived" or that "anxiety is ontological; fear psychological." [28] To the extent that the latter statement means that fear is a response which is derived from a prior condition of anxiety, this condition being a universal human one, it can be understood and affirmed. But in chapter 4 it has already been shown that anxiety itself is derived from a prior condition of being in the infant, and that therefore it, too, is "psychological," while still recognizing the universality of its development.[29]

As indicated above, the most obvious concrete threat to one's self-affirmation is death. When a person becomes aware of nonbeing within himself through the anticipation of his own death, the anxiety which may have been latent is aroused and subjectively experienced. "This anxiety is potentially present in every moment. It permeates the whole of man's being." [30] Yet day by day anxiety is not experienced as conscious fear of death. Rather, the characteristic human form of ontological anxiety is anxiety about meaninglessness. If man might not be, then why is he? And why should he continue to be? What meaning is there in his life? [31]

Tillich confirms these views in more detail in another place. The anxiety which arises out of finite freedom can be distinguished in three ways, each of which is a way in which nonbeing threatens being.

[27] Ibid.
[28] Ibid.
[29] See pp. 96-104.
[30] Tillich, Systematic Theology, I, 193.
[31] Ibid., pp. 196, 210.

First, "nonbeing threatens man's ontic self-affirmation, relatively in terms of fate, absolutely in terms of death." [32] This is most basic and absolutely inescapable: "existentially everybody is aware of the complete loss of self which biological extinction implies." [33] The anxiety of death is the shadow which lies over all other anxieties and gives them their force; it reinforces the contingency of our being.[34]

Second, nonbeing "threatens man's spiritual self-affirmation, relatively in terms of emptiness, absolutely in terms of meaninglessness." [35] Meaninglessness refers to the loss of an ultimate concern, a central, organizing meaning for all of the other possible meanings of human life. Emptiness is produced when circumstances cut one off from creative participation in that which he had previously affirmed. Other things are tried and they do not satisfy. Emptiness and meaninglessness are actualized in man's estrangement, his sense of isolation of himself from that with which he feels he should be united, that which is beyond himself. Man's very being involves his relations to meaning. "He is human only by understanding and shaping reality, both his world and himself, according to meanings and values." [36] To lose meaning is to lose one's self, to be empty.

The third way in which nonbeing threatens man's self-affirmation is in the area of the moral, through the anxiety of guilt and condemnation. This has already been discussed in the preceding chapter.[37]

[32] Tillich, *The Courage to Be*, p. 41.
[33] *Ibid.*, p. 42.
[34] *Ibid.*, pp. 43-45.
[35] *Ibid.*, p. 41.
[36] *Ibid.*, p. 50.
[37] See pp. 122-23.

Critique

The existentialistic writers have performed the service of portraying openly and honestly the dynamic forces at work in the existing individual as a result of their very perceptive analysis of the human being. They have laid bare schemes of self-deception and evasive behavior and labelled them for what they are. They have moved to the forefront man's experience of freedom and its awesome responsibility. They have pushed behind stated motivation to the universal anxiety which pervades human existence and have seen its power to move a person into a certain style of life. They have forced the reader to acknowledge the reality of his own death, the reality and basic nature of his anxiety about it, the utterly shaking power of this anxiety to disrupt one's life, and have lifted up inauthentic styles of life as being forms of living death, or forms of death within life. They have shown how man stands alone in the moment of his decision about the present meaning of his life in the face of his ultimate death, and how his full life, his authentic existence, depends upon this lonely decision.

Their failure seems to lie not so much in their inaccuracies in the description of the life of the maturing person, but in their failure to account developmentally for anxiety and the forms of behavior which come into being as a method of coping with the intolerable pain of this affect. Actually, their *description* of what is termed ontological or existential anxiety and the concepts connected with it is upheld by the observations of those in the field of the behavioral sciences.

CLINICAL OBSERVATIONS OF EXISTENTIAL ANXIETY

Anxiety and the Loss of Meaning

Viktor Frankl. Frankl places the necessity for meaning at the heart of man's life; the search for it "is the primary motivational force in man." [38] He traces the arousal of anxiety of an unmanageable degree to the failure of a person to find meaning in life and to assume responsibility for his existence. Back of every neurotic anxiety lies existential anxiety.[39] Existential anxiety is the "fear of death and simultaneously fear of life as a whole." [40] A person seems to have this fear of life when he has lost his central value or values, and the loss of value is experienced as the meaninglessness of life. As a result of the failure to find meaning, to create value for oneself, the person feels guilty toward life and there is anxiety toward life and death.[41] "As soon as life's fullness of meaning is rediscovered, the neurotic anxiety (to the extent that it is existential anxiety) no longer has anything to fasten on." [42]

The question of the meaning of life is not to be answered in general terms but rather in terms of the specific meaning for a particular person at a given time.[43]

Erich Fromm. Fromm agrees concerning the need for meaning, and this is precisely man's central problem. The perpetuation of his primary ties block his full human development, his reason, his widening and deepening relationships, his self-determining capacities. Yet within these primary ties is security. Here a person has a structured place. He is relatively safe. With the breaking of the primary ties and movement toward individualization as a person, there is a growing sense of isolation, insecurity, doubt concerning one's place in the universe

[38] *Man's Search for Meaning* (Boston: Beacon Press, 1962), p. 99.
[39] *The Doctor and the Soul* (New York: Knopf, 1955), p. 209.
[40] *Ibid.*, p. 210.
[41] *Ibid.*, pp. 209, 213.
[42] *Ibid.*, p. 214.
[43] *Man's Search for Meaning*, p. 110.

and the meaning of one's life.[44] To put it another way, there is increasing anxiety as a result of separation and the loss of meaning. His basic need is "to find an answer to the question of the meaning of his existence and to discover norms according to which he ought to live." [45] It should not be thought that meaning implies certainty. There is no given certainty to life. Yet meaning can be created by man as he allows his own powers to be expressed in productive living, in relatedness and love.[46] Broken away from primary ties, but without relatedness and love, a person feels alone and powerless, thus threatened, anxious. This is the condition of every person.[47] As one seeks to find security, escapes from anxiety, in various values and meanings, it is clear that everything which threatens these central, vital interests threatens the whole person and is experienced as anxiety.[48] There are a number of avenues of escape from the individual freedom which produces anxiety, but a number of them are the types of evasion and denial which Heidegger would term inauthentic: authoritarianism, destructiveness, automaton conformity.[49] The anxiety of one's free existence is effectively met by a person's relating

himself spontaneously to the world, in love and work, in the genuine expression of his . . . capacities; he can thus become one again with man, nature, and himself, without giving up the independence and integrity of his individual self.[50]

[44] *Escape from Freedom* (New York: Holt, Rinehart & Winston, 1941) pp. 35-36.
[45] *Man for Himself* (New York: Holt, Rinehart & Winston, 1947), p. 7.
[46] *Ibid.*, pp. 45, 96.
[47] *Escape from Freedom*, p. 29.
[48] *Ibid.*, p. 181.
[49] *Ibid.*, pp. 141-206.
[50] *Ibid.*, p. 140.

Henry Lindgren. Lindgren, the psychologist, links awareness of death and lack of meaning as the root of anxiety. He
states that basic anxiety is an "unconscious awareness" that
we are alive only temporarily; it is always lying behind all conscious awareness. There is a constant inner tension growing
out of the "fear that some day we shall cease to be the persons
we are." [51] Again he says: "somewhere out in the future lurks
death—the end of ourselves as we know ourselves." [52]

The basis of this fear is in the human character of a person.
Because he is a self, things tend to be interpreted in the light
of "self-reference." "All anxiety-provoking situations raise this
question, 'What is going to happen to me?' " [53]

The "self-reference" perspective forms the link between the
threat of death and the lack of meaning as productive of anxiety. One of the characteristics of being a self is the constant
organizing of experiences into a mental picture of one's self,
a self-concept. This is the framework out of which our own
behavior and that of others toward us and new experiences are
interpreted. Behavior and experiences which do not tend to
substantiate the self-concept tend to be responded to as threatening. This is simply to say, if they do not make sense, have
meaning to the person, within the framework of his self-
concept, they are anxiety producing.[54] Therefore, "anxiety is
caused by an absence of meaning—by meaninglessness, by
situations that do not make sense to us. . . . The antidote to
anxiety is meaning." [55]

This review of Frankl, Fromm, and Lindgren has sought
to demonstrate that sensitive professionals in the fields of

[51] *Meaning: Antidote to Anxiety* (Camden, N. J.: Thomas Nelson,
1956), p. 16.
[52] *Ibid.,* p. 60.
[53] *Ibid.*
[54] *Ibid.,* pp. 54-55.
[55] *Ibid.,* p. 34.

psychology and psychotherapy have presented material based upon clinical observation which supports the statements of existentialistic philosophers and theologians concerning the relationship between loss of meaning and anxiety, and that the concept of one's own death is related to loss of meaning.

Anxiety and Human Finitude

Human finitude is most powerfully and finally understood in the reality of death. It has been seen that existentialistic philosophers and theologians emphasize death as having a crucial role in human existence, and that the fear of death is one of the central forces in existential anxiety. Although psychoanalysis operates traditionally within a different conceptual framework than that of existentialism, it does confirm from a clinical point of view the universality of the fear of death and links this fear with the anxiety level of the individual person.

Freud felt that the fear of death was related first to the infant's feeling of helplessness in the face of intense instinctual drives at the absence of the mother, and second, at the later separation anxiety of castration fear. The situations are analogous.[56] The fear of death is a result of the final transformation of this same separation fear, the fear of the super-ego, when the latter is projected outward onto the powers of destiny.[57] This fear, Freud felt, was immediately met with the defense mechanism of denial and became the source of the idea of immortality.[58]

Chadwick agrees with Freud that the original source of anxiety is the infant's perception of his helplessness, the feel-

[56] Freud, *Standard Edition*, XX, 130.
[57] *Ibid.*, 140.
[58] *Ibid.*, XIV, 294-95.

ing of threat to the ego, and the understanding of death as "the power over which we have no control." [59]

It is this idea of the extinction of the ego, which is the most intolerable factor in the conception of the fear of death. The greatest difficulty presented to the mind is to realize a negative condition, a state of non-existence of the self or the non-continuance of existence in relation to the outside world.[60]

Zilboorg verifies the universality of death anxiety in a very explicit statement: "No one is free of the fear of death." [61] It is the basic fear which lies behind every feeling of anxiety and fear in any situation of danger.[62] Fear of death is the affective aspect of the effort of the organism to preserve itself in the face of dangers that threaten life. Zilboorg's thesis is that of necessity this fear *must* be repressed in order to allow the person to live comfortably and function properly. He recognizes that under repression it still operates unconsciously and must be allowed some outlet.[63] At this point Zilboorg differs from the existentialist writers who have spoken of the necessity of the anticipation of death, the courage to accept this limitation as a part of oneself. He expresses what he feels to be the proper attitude:

We must maintain within us the conviction that we are stronger than all those deathly dangers, and also that we, each of us who speaks of himself in the first person singular, are exceptions whom death will not strike at all.[64]

[59] Mary Chadwick, "Notes upon the Fear of Death," *International Journal of Psychoanalysis*, X (1929), 323.
[60] *Ibid.*, pp. 329-30.
[61] Zilboorg, "Fear of Death," p. 466.
[62] *Ibid.*, p. 465.
[63] *Ibid.*, p. 466.
[64] *Ibid.*, p. 468.

He does not mean, of course, that a person can come to the place where he can deny death intellectually, but he feels that an effective repression of the affect can so separate the verbal admission of one's own death from the affect that "he does not really care. He is having a good time with living, and he does not think about death and does not care to bother about it." [65]

Wahl agrees with the existentialist writers, though, when he states that it is possible for a person, without total repression of the affect, to see death as a completion of a pattern, spend one's life without fear, live creatively and productively and with satisfying relationships, "to integrate and accept the thought that his self will one day cease to be." [66] This is a possibility which is built on the foundation of a childhood where anxiety was induced only to a minimal level, where there was a strong, positive relationship of love and trust with adequate, nonanxious parents.

The child who is strongly dependent upon his significant adults for his security and his conception of himself as a worthy and adequate person is capable, if they meet these needs, of integrating the concept of "not-being" if his parents can do so.[67]

Wahl seems to have built upon the conceptuality of Klein, who spoke of how the increase of love and trust and the production of happy experiences diminished to a minimum the separation anxieties of the infant. These experiences with the parents become incorporated as "good objects," they serve immediately as the positive forces which allow the ego to face threatening experiences without acute fears of destruc-

[65] *Ibid.*, pp. 470-71.
[66] Wahl, "The Fear of Death," p. 323.
[67] *Ibid.*, pp. 322-23.

tion, and they remain a part of the ego to serve the same purpose from that time on.[68] These internalized "good" experiences become the resources which enable a person to face successfully the mourning-anxiety cued off by the death of a love-object, when one's own inner world is perceived as in the process of disruption.[69]

The person with incorporated "good objects" will be able, according to Wahl, to discuss openly the possibility of his own death and live creatively and freely with this possibility. Here, then, is presented by psychoanalysis the foundation for the "courage to be" in the face of one's nonbeing and the openness toward death of which Tillich and Heidegger have spoken.

Other analysts have also observed the universality and the motivating force of the fear of death.[70] It is at once clear that the psychoanalysts have some differences among themselves in the exact language which they use to refer to the origin and the intrapsychic dynamics of the fear of death and, to some degree, the way in which it should be handled. Nevertheless, these therapists are in general agreement concerning the reality of death anxiety, its universality, and its influence as a strong motivation in human life. It is also to be noticed that almost all of them have spoken of it in the same terms and in the context of the identical origin as simply separation anxiety. In spite of their own theoretical differences, it is still possible to accept their clinical observations of the fear of death as supportive evidence for the ideas presented in existential

---

[68] Klein, "Mourning and Its Relation to Manic-Depressive States," p. 128.

[69] *Ibid.*, p. 135.

[70] Bernard Brodsky, "The Self-Representation, Anality, and the Fear of Dying," *Journal of the American Psychoanalytic Association*, VII (1959), 105; Monsour, "Asthma and the Fear of Death," pp. 59-61; Simmel, "Self-Preservation and the Death Instinct," pp. 165, 167.

philosophy and theology concerning the universal operation in human life of anxiety, the central core of which is related to one's own death, the possibility at any moment of our own nonexistence.

The experience of freedom. On the whole, the existentialists and the psychoanalysts differ from one another concerning the source of anxiety in freedom on the one hand or in a determined manner on the other. This is certainly not the place to revive the well-worn but still unresolved question of determinism *versus* freedom. It may well be that a major difficulty is still a semantic one. The important point is that they both point to the universality of anxiety, and they both speak of death anxiety. If it is inevitable, then the question of whether it is necessary becomes only a word game. One does not *have* to respond to his awful sense of freedom with anxiety; he merely always does. The parents do not have to be anxious in the presence of the infant and small child and be inadequate to meet all of his needs consistently; it merely follows that in the ongoing pattern of life this is the way they *do* behave.

A dual recognition has to be made. First, it is obvious that the infant comes into an interpersonal situation not of his own choosing and without the ability to select freely the stimuli to which he will give attention. The rudiments of selfhood as presented in chapter 3 are given to him by the behavior of his parents toward him. In this context there develops an interpersonal self who cannot escape perceiving and responding to threats to himself in the form of separation from the significant others. There is anxiety prior to freedom.

Later, however, the developing human person begins to have experiences of choice and decision which he calls freedom. He is aware of responsibility concerning himself; he becomes conscious of his temporal finitude; he questions the

164

meaning of his existence; he fears death, annihilation of himself. In this context, too, he experiences anxiety. Yet as was indicated, this second level of anxiety is built upon the first, and the intensity of it is dependent not so much upon the reality of the threat, but upon the prior level of anxiety, although different and more newly learned stimuli cue it off. And, as the therapists have noted, even the fear of death itself arises out of the infant's situation of interaction with others.

EXISTENTIAL ANXIETY IN THE GRIEF-ANXIETY REACTION

Anxiety defined and elaborated in existential terms has been observed as an integral part of the grief reaction by a number of writers. Interestingly, the academic psychologists have not made these observations. Waller, the sociologist, feels that it is important not to overlook the fact that the death of a person emotionally close to one is a reminder to the one left behind that he, too, must die, and that the bereaved person does appear to be acutely concerned about his own death.[71] Eliot, in the area of social psychology, has noted the reactions of the grief-stricken as including a loss of meaning in much that had previously seemed important and that there was a sense of emptiness and futility.[72]

It is not unexpected that practitioners and writers in the field of pastoral care would be more prone to perceive a sense of emptiness and meaninglessness and the question of one's own death and to develop an interpretation of these factors in relation to anxiety with more frequency than others. Certainly to do so is more in keeping with a theological orienta-

[71] Willard Waller and Reuben Hill, *The Family: A Dynamic Interpretation* (New York: Dryden Press, 1951), p. 486.
[72] Eliot, "Bereavement: Inevitable But Not Insurmountable," p. 653

tion than it is with the behavioristic-experimental approach of much of contemporary academic psychology.

Kean has observed as one aspect of the dynamics of grief "the reminder of one's own eventual death." [73] He has noticed that this response to the death of someone emotionally close is sometimes conscious, sometimes unconscious, but he states that the fear of death is an almost universal anxiety and that it raises the existential question, "Has life any meaning other than that which we as human beings put into it?" [74] If the answer to this question is in the negative, then death is threatening by seeming to annihilate everything that matters. This conclusion is warranted by the human experience which has been so clearly stated by the existentialists that when one reflects on the meaning of life he must also reflect on the reality of death and its relation to the meaning of life. Benda, a psychiatrist writing specifically for ministers, sees "the reality of death as the symbol of our finitude" as an element of the grief reaction which calls for our acceptance.[75]

Rogers, in viewing the needs of the bereaved, perceives that a sense of the unity of experience and the recognition of a purpose in life is of value in reducing the intensity of the grief reaction.[76] In other words, an increase of meaning produces a reduction of grief response. Or to reverse the statement, the lack of meaning would tend to increase grief. Rogers has made it clear, as chapter 3 sought to do in more detail, that relations with other persons and objects in the attempt to meet one's security needs produce the total context

[73] Charles D. Kean, *Christian Faith and Pastoral Care* (New York: Seabury Press, 1961), p. 105.
[74] *Ibid.*, p. 110.
[75] Clemens E. Benda, "Bereavement and Grief Work," *Journal of Pastoral Care*, XVI (1962), 9.
[76] William F. Rogers, "The Place of Grief Work in Mental Health" (Ph.D. diss., Boston University, 1949), p. 87.

out of which a person operates as a person. These others are a significant part of the meaning of a person's life, and these persons and their meanings for one become literally a part of one's own self.[77] Thus, the loss of the other is interpreted as the loss of meaning which is the equivalent of the loss of one's self, the core of the affect of anxiety.

Irion is another who stresses that the meaningfulness of life can be described in terms of interpersonal relationships.[78] Therefore, whenever a relationship is broken one's system of meaning normally does not remain undisturbed.

Jackson confirms from his experience that the dynamics of one's understanding of his own finite nature are always involved in the dynamics of grief. "The fear of our own death lurks relentlessly in the back of our minds, and facing the mystery of death always opens to us the gulf of the frightening unknown." [79] Man's ability to understand his finite nature and to conceptualize it is the same capacity which leads him to seek for meaning and coherence in life's experiences. Jackson observes the loss of meaning as a symptom of grief. He then shows the relation of this aspect of grief to the individual's total value structure and concludes that if one's sense of life's total meaning encompasses present relations with others but also goes beyond them, then the death of these persons is not seen as the end of all meaning nor is it interpreted as some ultimate threat to the person himself.[80]

Death of a Significant Other as a Stimulus to Existential Anxiety

The dread of death is a universal human emotion. It is related to the necessary search for meaning in life. Fear of

[77] Rogers, "The Pastor's Work with Grief," *Pastoral Psychology,* XIV (September, 1963), 19-20.
[78] Irion, *The Funeral and the Mourners,* p. 26.
[79] Jackson, *For the Living* (New York: Channel Press, 1963), p. 23.
[80] Jackson, *Understanding Grief,* pp. 114-21.

death and lack of meaning combine as central characteristics of what has been referred to as existential anxiety, present in all persons at all times. It cannot be removed. However, it can be evaded, and people do this in varying degrees by mechanisms of denial, repression, sublimation. Although what is called existential anxiety is a motivating force in human behavior to some degree at all times, only on occasion does it break out as overt anxiety. One of these occasions would seem to be when someone very closely related emotionally dies. Usually, as Heidegger has so well said, society gives to the individual the thought forms and behavior patterns that he needs to depersonalize death and to separate oneself from it temporarily. A person is deceased, or departed. He is asleep. The cemetery is called "Slumberland," or even more neutrally, "Forest Park" or "Green Meadows." The preparation of the body is in the direction of making it look as lifelike, or as "natural" as possible. Deaths are reported by the news media in very matter of fact ways or as statistics. The emotional reaction of the public to an issue of *Life* magazine's presentation of the individual pictures of all the young men who were killed in one week in Viet Nam rather than the usual statement that "242 men were killed in combat last week" indicates the power of the personal to point up sharply our typical impersonal manner of handling violent death.

However, as Irion has perceived, evasion of this anxiety is made very difficult by the reality of the death of someone very close to a person, an event which tends to personalize death and stimulate the fear of his own.[81] It is personalized because the earlier process of emotional identification with the other means that the other lives as part of one's self, not completely separate from one, and his death cannot be seen in any way

[81] Irion, "In the Midst of Life . . . Death!" p. 48.

other than in terms of personal reference to one's own life.

It might be informative at this point to refer to Meissner's study of the responses of subjects to psychoanalytic death symbols. His hypothesis was built upon the concept of anxiety as being basically a fear of death. He noted that there was greater emotion present in the individual as measured by the galvanic skin response to those words which in psychoanalytic theory were symbolic of death than to those which did not have such symbolism.[82] If there is validity at all to his study at the point of there being a fear of death which can be stimulated by certain cues, it might well be assumed that the death of a person with whom one had identifications would be a considerably more powerful cue than words with death symbolism. Zilboorg has specifically stated the force of the death of another in breaking through defenses erected against fear of death: "Not until (a person) begins to lose members of his family and friends . . . does he come to grips with the fear of death by way of identification with those who were killed." [83]

Existential Responses to Death of the Other

It seems as if there would be at least three responses related to the arousal of existential anxiety which might be cued off by the death of an emotionally significant person.

Loss of meaning. First there is the question of meaning. This other, in whom there has been an emotional investment, is dead. In the relationship there had been meaning. It had been felt that indeed there was meaning in the life of the person. Now that he is dead, the question about the significance of the other thrusts itself to the fore. "He was of value to *me*. Was there, *is* there, any other value? Did his life really

[82] Meissner, "Affective Response to Psychoanalytic Death Symbols," p. 299.
[83] Zilboorg, "Fear of Death," p. 471.

169

have the meaning attributed to it by me? Or has his life been without meaning?" This inevitably raises the additional question of the present meaning of one's own existence. "In light of the fact that I, too, shall die, is my life of permanent significance?"

Nonbeing. This leads to a second response. Man ponders the idea of what it must mean not to be. But he cannot think concretely about his own death under most circumstances. It is possible to observe the death of an other, but not of our own except as abstract thought. But when the other who dies carries with him to the death some of our own emotional investment, an extension of ourselves, this comes as close as possible to the experiencing of our own death. It brings into awareness the anxiety concerning death that is a part of every person through the affectively charged thoughts: "It *could* have been I. Why was it not I? Something in me *is* dead. I too *will* die. I will not *be.*"

Responsibility. A third possible response is that of the anxiety of responsibility for one's own life until his death. The question is not just that of one's own future death, but the anxiety concerning how his own life can be sustained without the emotional support of the one who is now gone. Life has been lived in relationship. How can it be lived fully and with meaning in separation? "I am left alone to be fully responsible for my own life, which is now empty."

Equivalence of Death Anxiety and Grief Symptoms

An illustration of the equivalence of symptoms between death anxiety and the grief reaction is afforded by a young woman who sought counseling. Her overt symptoms were those of acute anxiety attack; her subjective experience was that of intense fear, verbalized as fear of death. She was afraid that she was going to die. Except for the fact that no one whom she knew had died and that the total subjective experience was that of fear of death, the disorder ran a course which under other circumstances might have been called grief. There were feelings of loneliness, of being abandoned, depression and despair, periods of weeping, many times gasping, deep sighs, the swallowing of air, general shakiness, inability to eat or to sleep well, the expression of a feeling of emptiness and the loss of all meaning to life. She stated that there seemed to be no reason to live, although she usually moved on to say that she had not given up the hope that she could find a reason. After several weeks of counseling the symptoms gradually began to subside, although not disappear entirely. She began to eat and sleep better, have fewer and less severe feelings of depression and less weeping. After about ten weeks most of the symptoms had disappeared with the exception of occasional feelings of being alone, the question of the meaning of her life, and occasional thoughts about death. However, the thoughts, although somewhat disturbing right at the moment, were no longer accompanied by a disruptive affect of fear. Her adjustive behavior in the several weeks following seemed to show that the death anxiety was actually being resolved rather than simply repressed. In addition to the counseling relationship and important insights, she was developing a very meaningful affectionate relationship with a young man. In all of this she was finding a meaning for herself and the ability to live with the thoughts of death without a paralyzing fear. If someone had been able to observe this girl closely without knowing any of the subjective factors, he might well have judged the situation to be that of acute grief, with the gradual subsiding of grief symptoms with the passage of time and the attachments of new relationships and activities.

EXISTENTIAL ANXIETY CONCEIVED OF
AS A SEPARATION ANXIETY

Review of Relevant Concepts of Separation Anxiety

By way of a review of relevant ideas, reference should be made once more to the unavoidable learning of the anxiety reaction by every infant, arising from the anticipated fear of pain during the absence of the one upon whom he is dependent and upon whom he learns that he is dependent. Thus, the first basic anxiety is connected with separation from a significant other.

It should further be repeated that the attitudes and behavior of the other, and later others, are introjected as the original dynamic foundations of one's self. The developing self is interpersonal in its nature, and the absence of the significant other is primarily experienced as self loss.

It is also to be remembered that meanings are learned in the context of these affective relationships, and the language which facilitates the learning and communication of meaning is also learned in this same context. Although meaning can be intellectually formulated, its origin and force is not only emotional, but emotional-relational. Meaning is given and received in relationships. The breaking of relationship is the loss of meaning. But the breaking of relationship is also perceived as self loss, threat to self, with the response of anxiety being stimulated. Therefore, the breaking of relationship involves a sense of loss of meaning and is simultaneous with the subjective anxiety.

Relation of Self Loss to Loss of Meaning

It remains to point back to the learning of the fear of death, which has been described as rising out of the affect of separa-

172

tion anxicty, and as being the ultimate threat of self loss. There is a sense of loss of meaning within the experience of anxiety because there is the sense of loss of the self which can respond to meaning, which can create and hold meaning. In separation there has been loss of a central value, actually one's own self, but in separation experienced as the loss of the extended self in the other. The symptom of the feeling of emptiness has more than symbolic meaning; there is an affective self loss. Something (in terms of emotional dynamics, meaning) which was there is no longer there. The loss of one's own self, of which the introjected other is a literal living force, through separation from the other is what the fear of death and loss of meaning are all about. In grief it is the reproduction of an early learned anticipation of pain to the self, experienced at the present because the process of stimulus generalization has led the person to make the same response to any form of separation from others, separation having been the original stimulus. Not the precise form of the separation, but the intensity of the infantile roots of the fear seems to be the determining factor. Anxiety is the painfully experienced alarm of threat to the self, and this alarm may be sounded by relationships with one's spouse that reactivate an unresolved Oedipus complex or by the poignant pointing up of one's own mortality by the death of an emotionally related person. It is the same alarm, the same anxiety.[84] Only the external stimulus, the contextual point of reference, is different in its conscious form of perception and in its symbolic formulation.

The Unity of Anxiety Experiences

Paul Pruyser, too, has reached the conclusion that existential or ontological anxiety as a separate and distinct category

[84] Hiltner, "Some Theories of Anxiety: Psychiatric," p. 35.

of affect is a myth. He makes a distinction between the affect of anxiety and the cognitive state which he believes is the primary meaning of what writers refer to as *existential* anxiety.[85] The latter he conceives of as a form of knowing concerning one's ontological status, his values, principles, ideals, and goals, his finitude. This type of definition, Pruyser feels, takes this supposed type of anxiety out of the psychological category.[86] As long as there is merely an intellectual discussion of problems and questions of life and death, it is only a philosophical exercise concerning existence. To the degree that there is genuine anxiety, it is existential in the sense that it is an affective experience of the existing individual,

felt centrally, demonstrated psychosomatically, experienced unpleasantly, and reacted to holistically. . . . Thus experienced, there is no categorical difference between existential anxiety and any other anxiety.[87]

The conclusion is in line with the concept developed in this book. Nevertheless, it would seem that Pruyser has made too sharp a distinction between values, principles, ideals, goals, questions of the meaning of life, the awareness of one's death, and the affective life. He has failed to express in his discussion the dynamic connection between the origin of separation anxiety and the interpersonal learning of meaning within the separation anxiety matrix and the learning of the fear of death and its relation both to separation and to meaning.

Hiltner agrees "that anxiety in the fundamental sense means one thing and not two or more." [88] His conclusion is based on

[85] "Anxiety: Affect or Cognitive State?" *Constructive Aspects of Anxiety*, p. 123.
[86] *Ibid.*, pp. 132-35.
[87] *Ibid.*, p. 139.
[88] Hiltner, "Epilogue," *Constructive Aspects of Anxiety*, p. 154.

the primary function of anxiety to warn concerning threat to selfhood. It makes no difference functionally whether the danger has to do with the evasion of a real external danger to the physical life of the organism or whether it has to do with questions of meaning, purpose, or finitude. "For (a person's) continuing existence, and his existence as a truly human being, the heeding of both signals is necessary." [89] At the same time, Hiltner makes very clear the concept which has been developed in this book concerning the priority of separation anxiety as being the source of affective experience, no matter what terms are used to describe the external circumstances or intellectual content of the experience, when he says, "I have never seen 'ontological anxiety' in pure concrete form." [90] But, not to overlook the integral relationship between meaning, sense of finitude, freedom and responsibility for oneself, he goes on, "and yet, on the other hand, I have never seen a disturbed mental patient without some trace of 'ontological anxiety.' " [91]

SUMMARY

Certain philosophers and theologians have raised questions and problems concerning man's existence in forms compatible with man's own experience of these matters of the meaning and purpose of life, freedom, responsibility, death, anxiety. These are termed existential or ontological questions and experiences, given by virtue of the very existence of the experiencing individual. At the core of existential anxiety are the threats to the individual implied in loss of meaning, the experience of emptiness, the anxiety of the responsibility for

[89] *Ibid.*, p. 155.
[90] *Ibid.*, p. 160.
[91] *Ibid.*

himself implied in his freedom, the dread of recognition of his own finitude, the possibility of his own nonbeing, fear concerning his own dying. Evidence for the reality of the fear of death and its significance as a motivating force in personality is drawn from the observations of the psychoanalysts. At the same time, other therapists and some psychologists have pointed to the central characteristic of man as being his search for meaning. It is not finally possible to separate the search for meaning for one's life from the recognition of the fact that one day he will cease to be, and in both of these the affect of anxiety as a warning of threat to the ego is involved.

A possible conclusion is that what is termed existential anxiety cannot be thought of as a different category of anxiety, but that the existentialistic writers are merely employing a method of expressing the universality of anxiety in man, its motivating power to lead one into inauthentic existence through the use of limiting mechanisms of escape and denial, its relationship to man's subjective experiences of freedom and responsibility, his loss of and search for meaning and self-affirmation, the basic question of his existence as a person, his fear of death, the annihilation of his selfhood.

But the affect which might be felt in the midst of such human experiences as the existentialists describe is the same affect of all anxiety, the fear of the loss of one's own self through the loss of or separation from a significant other, learned early in infancy and modified upward or downward in intensity depending upon the amount and quality of relationships of love and trust, or the lack of them, with the significant others in his life, and in the context of which he has learned his values and meanings and reason for being.

This is the very fear which is involved as the major aspect of the affective response of grief. It is separation anxiety in acute form cued off by the death of a person with whom one has been emotionally related. The issue of one's own death is raised since the death of an emotionally related person is perceived as the death of one's own self in two ways: the death of the extended self which had lived in the other and the death of that aspect of one's own self which was the introjected other. Thus, the person comes as close as possible within life to experiencing his own death. It is concrete, real, personal, close, frightening. This anxiety is a large element in the grief-anxiety reaction. It may be called existential anxiety for purposes of discussion because of the person's capacity to know himself as the one being threatened and his tendency to analyze his experiences and to grapple with the questions of meaning which are involved.

7
The Healing of Grief

Unless understanding leads to practical ends in human life, there would seem to be very little reason for merely going through the exercises of the mind. Therefore, all of the preceding discussion of grief should be productive both of further investigation and of the type of reflection upon the needs of the bereaved that will lead to their adequate fulfillment. In addition, the concept of grief as anxiety and the ways in which it has been elaborated should suggest a possible approach to preparation for this devastating experience. Hopefully, this

178

consideration, however briefly outlined, will contribute to a more constructive facing of the event and the more rapid healing of the distress.

A REVIEW OF THE CONCEPT OF GRIEF AS ANXIETY

This book has sought to fill the gap in the psychological literature dealing with grief by defining the reaction in terms of anxiety, an affect already quite familiar to psychiatrists and psychologists. In the past, definitions of grief which have been given or implied have usually fallen into one of two categories. First, grief is an emotion reactive to the death of an emotionally significant person (and to some degree at times of other major personal loss) and which is distinguishable from other emotions. Or, second, grief is merely a term used to apply to an interacting group of several identifiable emotions which have been stimulated by the death of a related person or by other loss. This book rejects the former usage on the grounds that no convincing case has been made for grief as a single emotion distinguishable from others. Such a distinction is not clear. Rather, within the framework of the latter definition, it has been proposed that the most significant affective element is anxiety, identical in its dynamics with any acute anxiety attack, with the external cue being the death of a person with whom one has been in emotional relationship. This thesis was developed by reviewing Freud's changing concepts of anxiety, taking his valid insights and then continuing to follow to its conclusion the interpersonal direction toward which he is seen as pointing. A theory of the interpersonal nature of the self was presented to replace Freud's exclusively somatic, instinctual assumptions as being a more appropriate theoretical

179

model for the understanding and discussing of anxiety as separation fear. The anxiety of grief is an experience of separation from or loss of a significant other, perceived as a threat to the life and integrity of the self.

Other emotions which have been observed and discussed in relation to grief, i.e., depression, guilt, and hostility, rather than simply accompanying grief, are much more integrally involved in it. Guilt itself is separation anxiety, and hostility is a universal response to another in an intimate emotional relationship, an affect productive of guilt. Depression is to be understood in grief as a common response to the painful affect of the threat of separation by the also painful turning of hostility inward upon the self.

What is termed existential anxiety by some philosophers and theologians, as well as some psychologists and psychotherapists, was also defined in terms of separation anxiety. This was relevant because of the observation that questions concerning the meaning of one's existence and the fear of one's own death were elements of the grief reaction.

IMPLICATIONS OF THE CONCEPT OF GRIEF AS ANXIETY FOR PSYCHOLOGICAL RESEARCH

Suggesting anxiety as the major affective element of grief provides a starting point in operational terms already current in psychology and for which instruments of measurement have already been designed and validated. At least here is something to work with. It might be, of course, that hypotheses based on this definition would not be supported by research results. If that were the case, data would still have been accumulated and analyses of these data might reveal the terms of other hypotheses. There is no question but what there is a need for sophisticated and imaginative psychological experimentalists to give effort to this area of human behavior.

It is to be noted that a major difficulty in the psychological investigation of grief is that of the sensitivity of the situation itself. Because of a basic human concern for the privacy of the feelings of others at the time of and immediately following the death of a person to whom they were emotionally related, investigators have hesitated to move in with a battery of tests, questionnaires, movie cameras, and tape recorders.

This does not mean that no one observes the grieving individual or that he cannot or does not communicate with anyone else. It is simply to recognize that those who are most likely to be present will also be to some degree emotionally involved in the situation. This is true also of the minister and the physician, although one might hope that these two professionals might be helpful coworkers in research in this area and that they might be the most reliable sources of the greatest amount of material. The exception to this would be, of course, the grieving person himself. The difficulty remains, however, that this is not the time that we try to get people to perform in experiments. Yet it would seem possible within a short time after the death to approach the bereaved person in a straightforward manner, explain the need to understand grief, and seek his cooperation in sharing his feelings and reactions as completely and honestly as possible.

This procedure would not be without its many inadequacies. It is not a controlled situation. There is not the direct observation of the person at the time of the most intense expression of feeling. There are emotional barriers to be considered. But it is not inconceivable that with the proper introduction, sensitivity to the person, and honest approach, persons still undergoing grief would cooperate with reasonable requests which would contribute to a body of knowledge concerning the reaction, and which might very well contribute to the process of healing for themselves. Certainly they do other things in response to many people's requests which are less reasonable and relevant.

THE NEED FOR HEALING IN GRIEF

Anyone who has ever experienced the pain of grief could hardly be so insensitive as to ask the question concerning the need for healing. The most obvious reason growing out of the feeling of distress is simply that it hurts. It hurts desperately. Agony cries for relief. Normal life is disrupted. There are sharply unpleasant emotions, physiological distress, an inability to think clearly, a sense of the loss of meaning, the inability to perform one's usual job and engage in useful projects, a lack of enjoyment in activities that formerly produced pleasure. No one wants to live this way. We naturally seek healing.

The Normal Grief Reaction and Grief Work

Several observers have described the normal reaction of grief and the process of healing which is referred to as grief work.[1] The immediate reaction to the death of an emotionally significant person is most typically some form of denial, an unwillingness to accept the reality with one part of the mind even as it is apparent to another part. Some type of emotional anesthesia is usually operative, and the person may appear to be stoical, dazed, or confused. Within a short period of time there is usually weeping, from moderate to the point of loss of control and even collapse. The intensity of pain sets in, and great waves of emotion seem to sweep over a person and threaten to

[1] Fulcomer, "The Adjustive Behavior," pp. 75-159; Lindemann, "Symptomatology," pp. 9-12; Oates, *Anxiety in Christian Experience*, pp. 52-55.

engulf him. One's total being is caught up in the experience and it consumes his whole time and energy: the emotions, the physiological accompaniments, and the thinking processes, all react to or focus on the deceased and the sense of loss.

Clayton's more recent study of the normal grief reaction indicated only three symptoms which were reported by over 50% of those interviewed within a short time after they experienced the death of a close family member: depression (87%), sleep disturbances (85%), crying (79%). Other frequently mentioned behavioral reactions were: difficulty in concentrating (47%), loss of interest (42%), anxiety at tacks (36%), irritability (36%), and tiredness (29%).[2] No striking differences were found when symptoms were related to the variables of age, sex, length of illness of the deceased, or family relationship.[3]

Gradually every aspect of this condition will normally diminish. The body makes its readjustments to its normal functioning. The intensity of the emotion diminishes, and later even disappears, except for periods of reoccurrence. The mind begins to be able to give increasing attention to other people and other concerns. Experience would lead us to expect approximately a six-week extent of time in order to see movement from the first reactions through the transitional period of diminishing intensity into the phase of constructive readjustment, the repatterning of life without the presence of the deceased and without the initial crippling reaction. Clayton's findings as a result of follow-up interviews showed that those persons who sought to date the beginning of their noticeable improvement designated the period six to ten weeks following

[2] Paula Clayton, Lynn Desmarais, and George Winokur, "A Study of Normal Bereavement," *American Journal of Psychiatry,* CXXV (1968), 171.
[3] *Ibid.,* p. 176.

the death.[4] To be sure, the six-week or even ten-week period does not mean the end of it all, nor should this time standard be rigidly applied to every person.

Although after the initial periods of denial, depression, regression, and withdrawal, there should be within a few weeks a movement in the direction of acceptance of reality, a lifting of mood, contemporaneity and relevance of response, and the reestablishment of more normal communication patterns, individual differences must always be taken into account. The movement of each person within grief work in regard to the various aspects of his life which have been affected must be judged not by a single rigid objective standard which is somehow universally normal, but by the criterion of his own usual personality and pattern of responses.

Most men in our culture are not observed continuing to have frequent periods of deep weeping beyond a few weeks after the death of someone very close to them. Probably more do than are observed. Our society has saddled men with a heavy burden in its expectation of the masking of emotions of sorrow and affection and tenderness. The tendency to inhibit such emotions is built into many men on an unconscious level as a result of this cultural expectation and they struggle to control them and not give expression to them too openly when they are consciously felt. But all men are not this controlled. Some are far more overtly expressive of their emotions than others. Therefore, when a man of this sensitivity and expressiveness of emotions lost his wife of many years, he found himself continuing to have long periods of weeping several weeks following her death. He could not even speak of her without his voice breaking and having the feeling of choking. He sought

[4] *Ibid.,* p. 174.

counseling, judging himself by what he understood society's standards to be, and questioning whether by those standards he was having an "abnormal" reaction. The point is, society's expectations and standards of behavior cannot dictate each individual's responses. His reactions were not "abnormal" for him. Within a few more months, even though the emotional pain was still frequent and intense, and some expression of this being made, there were fewer times of weeping, he could speak with greater control, he resumed his usual schedule of work and activities. There was no "special" counseling needed, just someone to help him understand what was going on in his own life and to keep check from time to time to be certain that progress was being made.

The grief reaction itself carries with it that which in most circumstances tends to produce its own healing. These healing forces are both the intrapersonal mechanisms and the social forms: the talking about the deceased, the decision-making necessary for the funeral, the social and religious customs, attentive care from other persons. Because of the resources of the normal human personality and the other persons in relationship with the bereaved, approximately six weeks will see most people moving back into much of their usual pattern of vocational responsibilities and social relationships, and carrying on with commitments of various kinds with an increasing degree of effectiveness. Another six weeks, or a total of about three months, is the time span within which most of the task of readjustment will take place.

In Clayton's investigation, twenty-seven of the forty initial bereaved persons were interviewed a second time one to four months later, all but one being within three months. At this time, 81% were improved, judging on the basis of the reduction of specific symptoms, 15% stated that they felt better in spite of the persistence of symptoms, and only 4% were worse.[5] The percentage of those reporting depression dropped from 87% to 12%, sleep disturbances from 85% to 27% and crying from 79% to 12%.[6] This certainly should not be taken to mean that reoccurrences of emotional pain will not take place. Over the years many things, such as personal belongings, anniversaries, special events, will have the power to stimulate the memory, reactivate the sense of loss, and stir the emotions, even to the point of weeping. Still, in all, the process of grief work is taking place in a manner which brings healing to the person.

The Disruptive Power of Grief

Inadequate or incomplete grief work. Grief work does not always take place in the manner just described, however. Complicating factors within the grief reaction form barriers to the normal constructive process. Where these barriers are not removed, the powerful anxiety of grief and the other emotions associated with it remain active in the personality to affect both the moods and the overt behavior of the person. Deutsch has clearly pointed out that this situation is no different from that involving other emotions, all of which are continually striving for realization. She illustrates the fact that "unmanifested grief will be found expressed to the full in one way or another." [7] If not expressed directly, openly, and at the appropriate time immediately following the death of an emotionally significant person, there is the strong likelihood that its form of expression will be in ways destructive to the happiness of the bereaved. These emotions will be reflected through depressed

[5] *Ibid.,* p. 173.
[6] *Ibid.,* p. 174.
[7] Deutsch, "Absence of Grief," p. 13.

moods, behavioral responses such as irritability, rejection of the help of others, and suspiciousness, all of which tend to destroy relationships, and even, as we have already seen, physical illness. Lindemann has gone into some detail to list forms of morbid grief reactions, such as these just mentioned and others.[8]

Even though one might expect a lifting of mood within a few weeks after the death, a person who has already been more prone to periods of depression might be expected to take somewhat longer without having it considered to be abnormal. Yet even for this person there is some limit. If, for example, four or five or six months pass without any discernible progress in coming out of the depression, therapeutic intervention is called for.

A man and his wife were in an automobile accident. Both were injured, the wife more severely. Both were hospitalized. The next day in the hospital the man died of a heart attack. The wife was not told at that time because of her condition. A few days later, she was informed. Her immediate and not unusual response was that she, too, wanted to die. The minister who visited her, while undoubtedly not meaning to do so, was perceived by her as treating her husband's death and her grief feelings in a casual and even calloused manner. Bitterness toward this minister set in, and in the midst of her depression, self-pity. After her release from the hospital, she, too, began to have heart trouble, whether coincidental or as a result of identification with her husband it was impossible to tell. Three years later, when another minister visited her in the hospital where she had been taken because of severe angina pains, he found that she was still depressed. Investigation revealed that there had never at any

[8] Lindemann, "Symptomatology," pp. 12-16.

time been any relief from the original response of depression to her husband's death. She was still filled with bitterness and self-pity, and much of her way of speaking was one that would normally tend to push people away rather than to invite them to sympathy and constructive relationship. The new minister sought to give special attention and spent long hours seeking to facilitate the grief work that was never adequately done and to make up for the interventions thtat had never been made, but there was relatively little response. Even though her prior personality might have led others to expect a somewhat more intense depressive reaction to the death of her husband, at some time after the third or fourth month following her husband's death, someone should have noted that there had been no progress in grief work and professional intervention should have been provided for. The original inadequately expressed grief and the clumsiness and insensitivity of those who should have been facilitating her grief work had led to a condition in which her life was permanently impaired, for within another two years she died, depressed, unhappy, feeling alone.

A rather emotionally expressive man whose wife of many years died demonstrated the anticipated strong reaction. Not only did his family and friends expect him both to weep and verbalize more than usual, but they were not surprised when six weeks and twelve weeks went by and there did not seem to be observable improvement. Nevertheless, they began to be quite disturbed when after some ten months he was exhibiting the same weeping and choking which he had had at the time of his wife's death. He continued to brood, and his conversation was taken up completely with references to her and to his sorrow. However, through a mobilization of concerned persons and through conscious efforts on the part of others to help him break this pattern, after approximately a year he was able to begin to make considerable progress.

Other data point to the overall seriousness of the disruption of life brought about by grief expressed inadequately or left uncompleted. The successful handling of grief is clearly related to long-range mental health of persons. Paul and Grosser made a clinical study of fifty families with schizophrenic members and twenty-five families with at least one neurotic member. They reported that all of these families had one feature in common: "maladaptive response to object loss." [9] Even though the death of the emotionally significant person may have occurred many years before, the "affects and attitudes toward the lost persons had remained essentially unchanged and recent losses evoked similar reaction patterns." [10] Such a fixation of relationships and repetition of behavior inevitably influences present interpersonal adaptations, and "may produce a family style that is variably unresponsive to a wide range of changes." [11] Thus, unresolved grief is discovered to be an important dynamic factor in all of the disturbed families seen by this therapist. Therefore, the importance of the successful working through of the anxiety of grief at the appropriate time is seen to be a contribution to the later stability of the closest possible personal relationships, those within the family.

The significance of the healing of grief as a preventive of further disorder is also emphasized by the role which loss is understood as playing in later serious depressions. Related to this are the data concerning loss as a major dynamic in suicide. Moss and Hamilton, in a study of fifty patients who attempted suicide, discovered that the desire for reunion with a lost loved one was a predominant factor in motivating the attempt. In

[9] Norman L. Paul and George H. Grosser, "Operational Mourning," *Community Mental Health Journal*, I (1965), 340.
[10] *Ibid.*, p. 341.
[11] Paul, "The Use of Empathy in the Resolution of Grief," *Perspectives in Biology and Medicine*, XI (1967), 161.

contrast with forty per cent of a control group of potentially suicidal persons, ninety-five per cent of the experimental group had suffered the loss of an emotionally significant person.[12] Other studies corroborate these findings, and many psychotherapists report their experiences with those individuals whose existence as persons is so closely bound up with the life of another that when the other dies, suicide, rather than being death for them, is actually seen as the way to life, the attempt at reunion. Where this is expressed as a part of the grief reaction, immediate therapeutic intervention is necessary. The healing of grief is imperative in order to save the physical life in order that the person might move toward his fulfillment as an individual.

The use of drugs in grief. The question should be raised concerning the not infrequent practice on the part of some physicians of administering sedatives to the grief-stricken just as soon as any of the overt signs of the anxiety which the bereaved are experiencing begin to be exhibited. Too often it has been observed that persons have been rendered incapable of thinking clearly or feeling acutely, which, of course, is precisely the job of the drug and the intent of the physician. However, it should be emphasized that it is not inherently detrimental to a person to experience anxiety in a conscious manner nor to express it openly in whatever forms are given to the person by his previous learning. In fact, it is this very awareness of pain which stimulates the acts which can reduce the affect itself, reducing the pain as a by-product, in contrast with a drug's merely reducing the person's feeling of the pain, whose source remains. Certainly there are occasions when acute anxiety is so intense that it borders on panic and

[12] Leonard Moss and Donald Hamilton, "The Psychotherapy of the Suicidal Patient," *American Journal of Psychiatry,* CXII (1956), 814-15.

can have rather swift destructive effects, as the personality then seeks for drastic survival measures in the attempt to keep from being overwhelmed. In such instances, appropriate drugs properly administered by a physician can be protective, and therefore in the long run, a constructive step in the overall process. However, the indiscriminate use of sedatives, tranquilizers, and other drugs as a matter of routine medical practice in every situation of grief may unnecessarily mask the pain of anxiety, therefore preventing the beginning of necessary first steps in the healing process: the clear realization of the reality of death, the feeling of the pain, the weeping, the immediate talking about the deceased and the relationship.

When this is the case, true healing may be retarded, or even worse, not adequately accomplished at all, with the anxiety of grief remaining unexpressed in a direct way, but continuing to function unconsciously and producing the detrimental behavior previously described.

For these reasons, the inevitable pain and anguish of grief under any circumstances and the disruptive power of inadequate grief work, there is an urgency in seeing that grief work takes place in an effective way within a reasonable period of time. It should be clear by now that the urgency is not to be conceived in terms of an attempt to rush the process in an aggressive manner when it is necessary for time itself to be a factor in the healing. Time as such is always involved. Nothing of an artificial nature is being suggested, nor can the grief work be made easy. The urgency, though, should be understood in the sense that other persons around the grief sufferer, both lay and professional, should be alert to the necessity of the process's continuing to move in a positive direction.

THE PROCESS OF HEALING

In discussing the relevance of the theory that grief is essentially acute anxiety whose basic force is separation fear and that it is best understood in terms of an interpersonal theory of the self, it is not assumed that something entirely new in the process of healing or in therapeutic or pastoral technique will be contributed. Rather, it is hoped that new understandings or different interpretations might clarify the meaning of the interpersonal relationship and the intrapsychic processes involved. Grief work must always be viewed in the light of the meaning which personal relationship has for the sustaining of the life and integrity of the self.

Anxiety as Motivation for Change

The first thing to realize then is that within the situation of grief-anxiety itself there are positive affective forces at work. Whitaker and Malone perceive the positive aspect of anxiety in psychotherapy and see it as occurring

in an individual who finds himself in an interpersonal relationship within the matrix of which he perceives the possibility of better organizing his affect (growing). In these instances, new and unorganized affect becomes mobilized for growth.[18]

In other words, the anxiety which is always experienced when one is confronted with his own potentiality, the outcome of which is uncertain and is thus a threat to the level of security which one has already attained, becomes the stimulus to move from one's present internal situation. This anxiety propels toward personal growth, the integration of new experiences, feelings, and meanings into the self concept,

---

[18] Whitaker and Malone, "Anxiety and Psychotherapy," p. 168.

thereby strengthening and enlarging one's self. Such positive anxiety is "commensurate with (the individual's) intuition of the potential depth of the interpersonal relationship with a particular (person)." [14] With this understanding of the positive aspects of anxiety, it is clear that it not only plays a significant role in the process of therapy but in all interpersonal situations. This needs to be emphasized in regard to grief, because in actual fact people do not normally go to a psychotherapist in their mourning and many do not even have the potentially helpful relationship with a clergyman. In these cases, grief work needs must be met by other members of the family and friends or by other professionals, such as the physician or funeral director, who, by the particular nature of the situation, may be involved.

That others have seen "constructive aspects of anxiety" is demonstrated in a number of writings. Although some within the field of psychology and psychotherapy would not accept the language with which the idea is communicated, one should not overlook the insights of these views. Kierkegaard expressed it: ". . . only the man who has gone through the dread of possibility is educated to have no dread." [15] Only the person who has looked with fear into the abyss of nothingness can rise above that which is truly anxiety producing in life. Anxiety is the teacher that enters into one's life, "searches it thoroughly," and pushes toward the rooting out of the insignificant and the trivial.[16] "Then when the individual is by possibility educated to faith, dread will eradicate what it has itself produced." [17] Through anxiety a person learns that his security is not in the finite and the transient, and therefore

[14] *Ibid.*, p. 169.
[15] Kierkegaard, *Concept of Dread*, p. 141.
[16] *Ibid.*, p. 142.
[17] *Ibid.*, p. 143.

may become capable of moving beyond dependence on these things. This movement is brought about by what Kierkegaard terms "faith," which in its dynamics are those dynamics of trust and security in meaningful relation with another.

Berthold differentiates between neurotic and creative anxiety, and assumes that one differentiating factor is the intensity, the creative aspect of anxiety disappearing when a certain high intensity is reached.[18] Anxiety is seen as being the "child of love" and "the mother of the drive to know." [19] This does not deny morbid elements and possibilities, but it is to affirm that there are also creative and constructive roles which anxiety can play. Berthold builds upon, but goes beyond to interpret, Kierkegaard's ideas. The biblical story of Adam and Eve is utilized to demonstrate man's guilt-anxiety as they sought to hide from God. What they feared was punishment, and the greatest punishment to be feared, picking up Freud's clue, is that of separation from the loved object. Therefore, Berthold judges, "fear of separation implies the positive impulse of tenderness, love, longing *about* the loss of which one is anxious." [20] He recognized the criticism of his own position in that the positive impulse may not be a mature object love, and perhaps, this writer feels, not deserving of terms such as tenderness and love without some qualification, but the point is that when one feels anxiety, it is an anxious longing, a striving, thus a drive to seek some condition other than that one is in. This anxious striving can be utilized for therapeutic movement in any anxiety state, including grief. Although there may in instances be fear of relationship, the underlying drive is desire for relationship. The openness, warmth, under-

[18] Fred Berthold, "Anxious Longing," *Constructive Aspects of Anxiety*, p. 70.
[19] *Ibid.*, p. 71.
[20] *Ibid.*, p. 79.

standing and congruence of the therapist, the pastor, other professional or even nonprofessional, can be the means of reducing the fear and breaking the barrier blocking the constructive force of anxiety.

Talking and the Needs of the Bereaved

Talking is a fundamental element in the relational communication of psychotherapy and pastoral care. Something of its meaning for the situation of the grief sufferer should be noted.

The concept of the development of the self and the integral affective relation of the learning of language which was presented in chapter 3 show how language in the infant and small child takes shape as essentially a security measure: first, as a necessary means of communicating basic survival and physical comfort needs; second, as a means of winning and maintaining parental approval; and third, even when the child is alone, as a means of holding the parents emotionally near. In other words, since language is learned within the matrix of interpersonal relations within which anxiety as a painful emotional response is also being learned, oral communication is among the first learned mechanisms of anxiety reduction. Language is a learned means of overcoming separation.

The relevance of this form of the interpersonal function of language has clear implications for grief. Numerous observers have noted a tendency of many grief sufferers to talk a great deal, especially about the deceased and personal relationships with the deceased.[21] Various reasons for this talking have been given. When one reviews the needs of the bereaved, the role

[21] Lindemann, "Symptomatology," p. 10.

of speech as a primary method of expediting the processes involved can be seen.

Release of negative emotions. One need almost invariably mentioned by all observers is that of working through negative emotions, such as hostility and hate and guilt. It is certainly not a new idea that encouraging a person to talk about his relationships with another until his words flow without inhibition, carrying with them the full expression of emotion, is a usual method by which such abreaction is accomplished. It is now merely better understood how words have come in the first place to assume such an affective charge and that the speaking of the words becomes the expression of the self which speaks them. Speech becomes a substitute form of the emotionally charged acts that need to be performed, understood, and accepted. In grief this need must frequently be facilitated by another person. Although guilt may often be openly expressed, more often than not, as we have already seen, the emotions of hostility and hatred and aggression appear in disguised forms of irritability toward others or toward one's self, the latter either directly or as depression. In the instance of the overt expression of anger by the bereaved toward the deceased, the tendency of others is usually to react with shock and disapproval, pushing the distressed person into the greater anguish of suppression and increased guilt and confirming his feeling that the others really do not understand and are not supportive of him. A perceptive family member or friend, or clergyman or other professional, may help the others in the situation understand the inner dynamics of the bereaved to the end that their own emotions of irritation or anxiety in response not become entangled with those of the grief sufferer. Talking about the deceased and the relationship with him may be encouraged until the real emotions become clarified and articulated. Even in the case of the open expression of guilt, others too frequently seek to gloss over what the grief-stricken is seeking to reveal, thereby not only cutting off genuine confession on his part but making him feel all the more guilty. His full expression of emotions must be stimulated and facilitated in order that he might rid himself of the power of the negatively charged affect.

Affirmation of one's self. A second need of the bereaved which relates to the first and which is not defined clearly by other writers is that of affirming positive attitudes toward one self. In the midst of grief, separation fear, and its related components of hostility toward the deceased and guilt-anxiety, one common reaction is some form of self-punitive behavior. There are elements of depression, and not infrequently a lowered estimate of oneself. Sometimes it is observed that language is used to express the self-punishment in the form of self-accusation. But it is also possible to use language to reinforce positive attitudes toward oneself. Words become the means of reestablishing one's threatened and disrupted selfhood. Mowrer has elaborated the position that since words are learned in temporal contiguity with a relationship which provides at least a minimal protection and meeting of need, words take on almost immediately a secondary reinforcing value and become the instruments of reproducing such attitudes of love and protection toward oneself which were the attitudes of the ones in relation with whom the words were first learned.[22] Klein has indicated that upon the death of an emotionally related person, there is the feeling that the original introjected good objects have also been destroyed, so that the task which brings grief to a successful conclusion is not only the rein-

[22] Mowrer, *Learning Theory*, pp. 708-9.

197

statement of the loved object just lost, but also the bringing back to life within one's self these earlier good objects, the parents and their positive responses to the infant and small child.[23] Earlier it was pointed out that one common mechanism of defense against acute anxiety is that of regression and that regression may well bring with it the talking which seeks to hold the parents near. Therefore, it can be concluded that if speech for the small child is a method of keeping parents emotionally close, and if the task of mourning is to reproduce those early good objects which take the form within one's self of positive attitudes toward one's self, then talking is an available behavior which helps in the performance of this task. Words have value for the maintenance of the self.

Breaking libidinal ties. A third need as stated by almost all the writers is that of freeing one's self from bondage to the deceased, breaking the ties, the removing of libido from the lost loved object. This is not as harsh as it may sound. Lindemann points to the communication of remembered experiences with the dead person as being involved in the process of the necessary emotional break. He is speaking of this verbalizing as being the emotional equivalent of reliving the experiences.[24] Weiss has also referred to the process of breaking libidinal ties by concentrating on every object and situation associated with the deceased until one by one the bereaved is emotionally freed from them.[25] According to Weiss, grief is the conflict between uncontrollable desire for the loved person and recognition that the person no longer exists, between the inner world of needs and the outer world of reality, with the latter gradually taking

[23] Klein, "Mourning and Its Relation to Manic-Depressive States," pp. 125-53.

[24] Foster, "Grief," p. 10.

[25] Edoardo Weiss, *Principles of Psychodynamics* (New York: Grune & Stratton, 1950), p. 11.

over dominance of the ego.[26] The transformation of inner life necessary for healing comes about with the process of exploring verbally every aspect of the relationship with the deceased as concretely and fully as possible until the person can accept each one without the intense inner longing. The primary emotional support which makes this possible is the establishment of emotional rapport with other persons.[27]

A minister had been retained to perform the wedding of an older couple whom he did not know. The day of the wedding he received a call from the groom. With trembling voice the man said that the ceremony had been cancelled. His bride simply could not go through with it. The minister asked if he might see them in order to try to help them through this time of crisis, and assured that he could, he went to the apartment. There he discovered the couple in great emotional distress. The issue was soon identified. The woman was feeling unfaithful to her former husband, who had died several years earlier. How could she remarry? Several months later, however, the ceremony took place. The crisis of the first wedding day had forced an open reexamination and expression on the part of the woman of her relationship with her dead husband in such a way that she was able to be released from the ties which had continued to bind her to him and not allow her to be totally free to enter into close new relationships. Now, so freed, she was able to make without guilt the commitment to this present man whom she also genuinely loved.

This concept of the need for release from libidinal ties is not without its validity. Surely there is emotion which has been directed outward to the other and energy used in the affective relationship which must be withdrawn from that person by the

[26] *Ibid.*, p. 10.
[27] *Ibid.*, p. 11.

sheer fact of physical absence, genuine object loss, and which will need to be expended in some other manner. It is also clearly demonstrated in psychotherapy that language is affective and relational in its very nature, since processes referred to as abreaction and catharsis are the verbal reliving of emotional experiences and relations with others.

The resurrection of the deceased within the self of the bereaved. Less frequently mentioned by other writers than the need to accept the reality of the death of the other and to withdraw libido from the lost object is the even more pressing need to reaffirm the life of the deceased within one's own self. To the extent that persons have been emotionally involved with one another, making an affective investment in one another, to that degree they have made identifications of their lives. One's self has certain aspects of the life of the significant other as a living component of it. When the other dies, the self is perceived as threatened with death by the loss of the other. But the external event of the death of an emotionally significant other need not annihilate the self. Rather, the other which is within one can be reaffirmed as living as a part of one's self.

The first response to the death of an emotionally significant person is undoubtedly the perception of threat of death to one's own self and the protective mechanism of the denial of the reality of the death of the other. The first verbalizing may be seen as the regressive tendency to continue to hold the other near, to recapture his presence through words. But usually the process moves on to the revival of the life of the other within the self. This emphasis is made by several writers in contrast with the withdrawal of the libido theme of Freud and others. Abraham speaks of reaction to object loss by setting up the object within one's own ego through introjection. The psychological result is "my loved object is not gone, for I now carry it within myself and can never lose it." [28] In this way the interpersonal relationship is maintained even though the other be dead.[29] Klein, too, speaks of the preservation of the loved object, the necessity in mourning of reestablishing the loved person as an active force in the ego of the bereaved, along with all of the good objects which he felt he had lost.[30]

Oates has given sensitive expression to what takes place within the self in the first perceptions following the death of a significant other on through the process of mourning. He refers to the psychological "death, burial and resurrection of . . . selfhood in the process of grief." [31] For when the introjected other is understood to be alive within the self, the self becomes whole and fully alive again. The language which has been the communicative link with the other, in being heard by the speaker himself, carries with it the emotional life of the relationship and reinforces the internalized presence of the other.

Renewal of relationship. The fifth need of the bereaved, and again one which is named by almost every writer who discusses grief work, is to cultivate other personal relationships, to renew and deepen other old relations and to establish new ones. Klein suggests that the mourner is strengthened against the threat to his inner life by contemporary relationships with people he loves and trusts, who share his grief, and in the midst of whose care "the restoration of the harmony of his inner world is promoted, his fears and distress are more quickly reduced." [32] This follows logically, since the major dynamic of grief has

[28] Abraham, *Selected Papers*, p. 437.
[29] *Ibid.*, p. 438.
[30] Klein, "Mourning and Its Relation to Manic-Depressive States," pp. 143, 154.
[31] Oates, *Anxiety in Christian Experience*, p. 54.
[32] Klein, "Mourning and Its Relation to Manic-Depressive States," p. 145.

been defined in terms of separation anxiety. It is the fear of self loss which was learned parataxically with separation from the significant other that needs to be dealt with. Engel, as a psychosomatic specialist, follows up this insight with a suggestion to the medical team for treatment. If grief is reaction to an object loss, then the maintenance and replacement of objects ("persons in relation") must be considered an important factor in the healing process. Therefore, the medical team itself should not be reluctant to enter into the life of the grief-stricken in a personal way, entering into relation with him, becoming for him a significant object.[33] Schnitzer has observed that even though "friends may have nothing to say, their very presence with the bereaved when he feels that the world is empty and void, has its remedial effects." [34] Certainly this has been the traditional role of the minister as he maintains a personal contact with the bereaved during the entire mourning process. He is to be present to and for the other.

What all of this is saying is that the answer to the anxiety of grief (separation) is love (union). The Bible states it: "Perfect love banishes fear." (1 John 4:18 NEB.) Fromm has offered productive love, union, as the only final remedy for the major source of man's ailments, separation.[35] But communion cannot be conceived of apart from communication. Although there are many forms of nonverbal communication, and even the presence alone of certain persons at the time of grief-anxiety is its own powerful communication, the powerful affective content of words must not be forgotten.

The rediscovery of meaning. In a very real sense, to speak of the rediscovery of meaning is not to introduce a new topic in

[33] Engel, "Is Grief a Disease?" p. 22.
[34] Jeshaia Schnitzer, "Thoughts on Bereavement and Grief," *Reconstructionist*, CXXXI (1955), 12.
[35] Fromm, *Man for Himself*, pp. 97-98.

addition to those which have already been discussed. It is primarily the using of another set of terms to refer to the process. Without these other needs being fulfilled, it is impossible to talk about the meaning of life. If these other needs are not met, words about meaning will lack adequate force to produce meaning itself.

This is another way of saying that meaningful sounding words are not the equivalent of the meaning of life. Nevertheless, once these needs are in the process of moving toward fulfillment, the human being naturally seeks to express his perception of his experiences in some coherent way. This, too, is a need. The conceptualization of what is taking place could properly be stated as the search for meaning, and the completion of the process the rediscovery of meaning.

The manner in which the death of a person with whom there has been a close emotional relationship produces a sense of emptiness and loss of meaning by way of the experience of self-loss has been traced in the previous chapter.[36] In addition, man has been described as a being for whom the search of meaning in life is central. According to Frankl it is a primary motivation.[37] We cannot really exist as fully human without a sense of coherence, purpose, values, and an understanding of our own roles in the larger life about us. When all of this is challenged by the death of someone who has been involved in the production of meaning in our lives, there is the sense of threat, the rise of anxiety which we call grief. The rediscovery of meaning brings with it the reduction of anxiety, in this instance, the healing of grief, since it was the loss of meaning which contributed to the rise of anxiety in the first place.[38]

The rediscovery of meaning, then, is to be seen as a process

[36] See pp. 172-73.
[37] Frankl, *Man's Search for Meaning*, p. 99.
[38] Frankl, *The Doctor and the Soul*, p. 214.

taking place on two levels. One is the emotional and relational: release of negative emotions, affirmation of oneself, the breaking of old emotional ties, the experience of the new life of the deceased within one's own life, the renewal of relationships. The other level is that of conceptualizing the process taking place, putting these experiences into meaningful symbols, verbalizing, which itself becomes reinforcing to the entire process.

It is impossible to escape the role of the famous triad: faith, hope, and love. Love we have already been talking about. Faith is not necessarily to be thought of in any traditional religious sense, although for many people this may be the most meaningful framework within which to understand the other meanings in their lives. However, it is clear that the popular definitions of faith as belief without evidence or the conviction directed toward some future event with the blithe spirit saying that everything will turn out all right are not relevant here. Tillich's definition of faith as ultimate concern is a useful clarification.[39] As such it is seen as an act of the whole being.[40] As act, the central force is that of present commitment, commitment to persons, causes, the meaningfulness of life, both because of the evidence for it *and* in the face of the apparent lack of it. This total commitment which affirms the meaningfulness of life and its activities and which engages the grief-stricken with other individuals and significant groups and causes is a necessary element in the healing of grief.

Also important is hope. Again, many would want to put this in some form of traditional religious language, and would even desire to speak of the relevance of hope for the grief-stricken in terms of life after death, the continuing life of the deceased, the anticipation of reunion at some time in the

[39] Tillich, *Dynamics of Faith* (New York: Harper, 1957), pp. 1-4.
[40] *Ibid.*, pp. 4-8.

future. Others find it difficult to conceive of the structure of life in this way. Nevertheless, for all persons hope can be understood as the possibility and openness toward the meaningfulness of the future which keeps faith alive and active in the present.

Karl Menninger has spoken of the reality and power of hope in expediting the therapeutic process. Hope can be distinguished from both expectation and optimism, the former being weak and the latter not related firmly to reality. Rather, it "implies process; it is . . . a going forward, a confident search." [41] Menninger develops the view of hope as a force within the person which has a sustaining function for human life. After citing experimental evidence with animals and anecdotal material concerning the role of hope in supporting human life, he states:

All of these things seem to me to support the theoretical proposal that hope reflects the working of the life instinct in its constant battle against the various forces that add up to self-destruction. [42]

Where such hope exists, faith may also live, and the discovery of meaning take place.

A beautiful and sensitive portrayal of this whole process of the healing of grief has been presented to us in the French film, *A Man and a Woman*. A chance meeting takes place between a man and a woman at the school at which both have children. In a drive back to the city they begin to know one another. Conversation reveals that the spouse of each is now dead. Occasion is given for them to be together again. Then they begin to seek opportunities to be together. Each speaks of the experience of grief.

[41] Karl Menninger, "Hope," *Pastoral Psychology*, 11 (1960), 15.
[42] *Ibid.*, p. 17.

The woman tells in detail of her great love and respect for her former husband. A series of flashbacks represent her talking to her new friend about her husband's virility, his lust for life, his appreciative love for her, and her response to him. Finally, there is the shock of his death in an accident while performing his job as a movie actor.

The man speaks with more reticence. He hesitates to pull out into the open and view and allow another to see details of a relationship that has been more painful. But finally the flashback expresses the sharing of the distress of his wife's mental illness and the horror of her suicide.

Through the intimate sharing of their grief with one another, the relationship between man and woman gradually develops. Each is affirmed by the other in the midst of sorrow; both positive and negative emotions are accepted. There is increasing appreciation for one another, and they discover that their former loneliness and emptiness is being filled by this new and meaningful relationship. Very tentatively they express their love for one another, not quite certain what this might mean for them, not quite free from their former ties. But the feeling is there. This new experience of love is joined by their very natural human passion, and in a delicately tender scene they meet one another in bed.

But while still in bed the woman has a strong feeling of guilt which turns her away from the man emotionally. Her experience is that of being unfaithful to her husband. The man senses that something has touched her and that the relationship has been affected. She seeks to express it to him. It is her husband.

At this point, the man does not fully understand. "But he's dead."

"Not for me."

Part of herself had been dead because of the death of her

husband. Yet, in spite of his death, part of his life remained active and influential within her. The paradox of life and death in the experience of grief is dramatically demonstrated in the intense conflict of this woman's emotions.

The man is obviously disappointed, not fully understanding, perhaps wondering about his own role in placing this barrier between them, unsure now of the future of the relationship, but still respecting her feelings.

She refuses his invitation to ride back to the city with him, taking the train instead. On the train, the screen pictures her review of the entire situation: memories of her husband, good and wholesome, her intense feeling of loss, the contributions of the new relationship to her life, her love for this new man who loves her, his acceptance of her, his respect for her, his sensitivity to her. In this process of reviewing, the old relationship is finally broken in such a way that she is released to live in the present and plan for the future, but without diminishing the reality of the past love and its meaning and the continued presence of the life of her husband within her own life. The guilt is looked at and forgiven. She understands her genuine love for her new man.

His sensitivity to her and knowledge of her has led him to imagine something of what she is going through and her very real need of him. So he has driven rapidly to her destination and is waiting for her at the station. She gets off the train. They see each other and rush into each other's arms. Nothing of value in the past or present has been destroyed, but grief has been healed.

REDUCING VULNERABILITY TO GRIEF

Alan Harrington has reflected that death is an unacceptable imposition upon the human race. The threat of it underlies much of human irrationality and disturbed behavior.[43] While some persons might want to use terminology other than the words "unacceptable" and "imposition," the emotional force which these words carry to us we accept as being true. Death, whether it be our own or that of someone with whom we have identified our lives, is the one human experience which the whole human race with all of its resources has sought to attack or evade. We can agree with Paul that it is seen by us as the enemy. (1 Cor. 15:26.) The very word "death" has come as a result of human experience to stand up against life. Yet, with all of our ingenuity, it remains inevitable that every person who reaches adulthood will at some time experience the death of someone who is very close to him emotionally and must face up to the reality of his own.

The implication of all that has been said up to this point in this book, though, is that grief is a crisis for which, like many others, we have some reserve of resources or to which we are quite vulnerable. Part of the value of any book dealing with any of the many human problems or areas of distress is its potential to stimulate a new and conscious awareness of the condition. This in turn should normally bring into being at least a beginning emotional readiness for the experience itself. By understanding fully *what* is going to happen at the time of bereavement, *that* it is going to happen, and *why* one's feelings and behavior take the form that they do, the person in addition to the original anguish will not be so shocked and terrified and rendered hopeless by the nature and power of his emotions. They still carry the pain, but a person can at least understand their universality and naturalness. Something of the mystery of why he feels this way is removed. Therefore, the feelings themselves should be somewhat less threatening to

[43] Alan Harrington, *The Immortalist* (New York: Random House, 1969).

him and it should be more possible for hope to be maintained even in the midst of grief.

To say that one can be made less vulnerable to grief ought not to lead to misunderstanding. There is no clever device by which to ward it off, no six easy steps by which the distress can be done away with. Death will remain death; the loss is a real loss; the pain still hurts. But a person may be better protected against the destructive powers which the anxiety of grief potentially contains and the severe disruption of life which it occasionally produces. A morbid grief reaction may be avoided. The future might be seen as remaining open. The person may even be able to come through his grief with greater strength of personality and with greater sensitivity to others in distress, thereby deepening the quality of all his relationships and adding meaning to his life.

Clarification of Present Family Relationships

From the material that has been examined here, a central need in the strengthening of the ego for grief would seem to be that of the clarification and improvement of our present relationships with those who are closest to us, our own family and any others whose lives have significant meaning for our own. The first aspect of this clarification is through increasing the amount and quality of our present communication. Such an increase in communication encompasses at least four areas. One of these is the expression of whatever negative feelings exist. Hostility, aggression, a sense of competitiveness, and other strong negative feelings should be brought out in their original form for all to recognize and for examination as to their source and meaning. Second, where there has been violation of others and a sense of guilt, confession needs to be made and forgiveness given and received. This does not necessarily mean that every detail of every violation of relationship, if these details are not already known, should be brought to light. There are undoubtedly occasions where some matters are better left secret. Nevertheless, the confession of guilt must be made in some form and forgiveness given and true reconciliation take place. Third, when an extremely immature dependence exists, whether this be between husband and wife, or the dependence of child on parent or parent on child, this immaturity of dependence should be recognized for what it is, brought into the open verbally between family members, and steps taken to reform the relationship on a mature level. The fourth area in which an increase in the amount and quality of present communication can always be developed is in the expression of tender feelings: love, appreciation, respect. One of two main handicaps in such expression exists in many people: the verbalization of love and tenderness without the support of acts which are confirming or the acting out of one's commitment to and appreciation for another without the verbalization. Both must exist for the fullest expression.

A second major aspect of the clarification of our present relationships within the family is closely related to what has just been said. We need to receive and accept affirmations of ourselves as they are given in the communications of others in their verbal and nonverbal affirmations of us, their acts of love toward us.

Klein has made it quite clear that the early incorporation of good objects is the best resource a person has for the maintenance and strengthening of his ego at the present time.[44] Therefore, the best way to strengthen one's self for the disruptive effect of grief is to have had in our infancy and early childhood parents who were warm and accepting and non-anxious and who met our needs in a relatively regular and

[44] Klein, "Mourning and Its Relation to Manic-Depressive States," p. 128.

effective way. To the extent that we had such parents and positive experiences, it would seem that these now incorporated good objects could be reinforced and made more lively by a conscious reflection on them from time to time. Recognizing that the early life experiences of many people have been less than ideal, few are totally devoid of such internal possibilities. Earlier reference has been made to Wahl's observations that the child in relationship with this kind of parent is capable of integrating into his being the concept of "not-being," and is thus given a source of strength in dealing with the event of death.[45] The internalized good experiences have a power to protect against disruption and to produce the healing of emotional pain.

The point to be made here is that the present acceptance of others' affirmations of us, to the degree that we are closely related to them emotionally and have relationships of mutual identification, both reinforces the good objects and is in fact productive of new ones.

This clarification of relationship, the increase of quantity and quality of communication, with those closest to us can be influential in the form and intensity of grief when one of them dies. The complicating factors of guilt and hostility have been handled within the living relationship day by day and therefore should not become a morbid or even greatly intensifying force in the anxiety of grief. A healthy interdependence, while hardly doing away with the pain of genuine loss, does not pose in grief the intensity of threat that is the experience of those whose relationship is symbiotic in nature. The mutual giving and receiving of affirmations within the relationship both lead to the liveliness of the good aspects of the other within the self and increase one's own sense of genuine self-acceptance and self-valuation.

[45] Wahl, "The Fear of Death," pp. 322-23.

211

This first consideration in strengthening for grief has to do with the present relationship with those whose death would normally be expected to produce severe grief, with the quality of the interaction with those persons which directly affects the form and intensity of the reaction to their death. A second consideration, however, is the need for the establishing of that quality of relationship with other persons who become resources of strength at the time of grief. While some of these are obviously other members of the family, the reference is also to larger numbers of friends whose affirmations of us become important to the maintenance of ourselves as persons.

A third major step in strengthening for grief is the active participation in those types of activities which can be renewed after the death of another with whom we have identified ourselves. A close sharing of life and activities should always be balanced by the development of one's own life as an individual through those activities, forms of recreation, organizational memberships, hobbies, and the pursuit of other interests which are expressive of and need fulfilling to our own particular personalities.

A fourth approach to strengthening for grief is one which encompasses the other three, but which holds them together in a unique way. No one way of stating it seems to be entirely adequate. The emphases up to this point have been of central and supreme importance. They should not be interpreted as being diminished by any further statement. Nevertheless, the total context of life within which a person views himself and his relationships and activities and their meaning cannot be overlooked as being reinforcing to them, and, even beyond that, as adding new dimensions to personhood. A view of life which both confirms the present meaning of persons and activities yet which is not totally dependent upon the present as ultimate can be an important resource in the living of the present, with or without the crisis of death and grief. Some persons would state this in terms of the development of an adequate philosophy of life, one which incorporates the reality of death both intellectually and emotionally into one's present being.

Even this, though, does not seem to be the most comprehensive form in which to express that which carries the greatest sustaining force for the individual. Somehow, what has been called philosophy of life here must not only encompass the meaning of present relationships and activities and include within it an emotional acceptance of the reality of death, but all of this needs to be developed and maintained within a community of persons. Such a community assumes that its members are supporting and affirming one another in the quest for the meaning of life and in significant caring for one another. The community also provides the symbols and rituals with the power both to strengthen the fellowship and, as one aspect of its strengthening function, to dramatize the major events, including the crises, of life.

The type of context usually provided by the religious community speaks of the meaning of life in terms which include death. It supplies the interpersonal reinforcements which contribute to the emotional acceptance of this reality, the opportunity for meaningful areas of life commitment, and a person-to-person caring for the dying person and the grief-stricken. Finally, the religious community provides the rituals which gather up and express in verbal form these life commitments, the faith, the hope, the love of those who share a common life style. In the funeral, these verbal expressions aid in the acceptance of the reality of the physical death and expedite the process of mourning through the stimulation of memories of the deceased. The funeral is both the symbol and the reality of the mobilization of the community to sustain those persons in distress as it pushes them along in their grief work.[46]

Apart from such religious communities, our society seems to be in short supply of formalized fellowships of persons which include all of the ingredients briefly mentioned here. However, this does not decrease the logic of genuine human need which would seem to speak its recommendation that such a community be sought and commitment be made to active participation in its fellowship, its quest for meaning, its causes, its rituals.

CONCLUSION

Grief: no one escapes. Yet with all our cumulative experience, our precise knowledge of its dynamics has been all too sparse, our methods of attempting to meet the needs of the bereaved have frequently suffered from this lack of knowledge as well as from our own anxieties, and our conscious preparation for that day when the grief is our own has been practically nonexistent. It is earnestly hoped that the concepts and approaches presented in this book will play some role in stimulating efforts to correct all three of these deficiencies in the understanding and facing of this extreme human distress, which has been or will be ours.

[46] For a more thorough discussion of the role of the funeral in the process of mourning, see Jackson, *The Christian Funeral: Its Meaning, Its Purpose, and Its Modern Practice* (New York: Channel Press, 1966), pp. 24-28, 33-36; Irion, *The Funeral: Vestige or Value* (Nashville: Abingdon Press, 1966), pp. 89-122.

index

Anxiety—*cont'd*
  universality of, 94-96, 146, 148-
    49, 154, 156, 158, 160-64,
    168, 172, 176
  See also Grief and anxiety; Grief
    as anxiety
Apathy, 105, 110-11
Atonement, 134
Authoritarianism, 158
Automaton conformity, 158

Bain, Alexander, 20
Becker, Howard, 137
Being, 122-23, 148-55
Benda, Clemons, 166
Bereavement, 12, 23, 24-28, 36, 51-
    52, 58, 63, 112, 137, 141, 208.
    See also Grief; Sorrow
Bergler, Edmund, 45
Berthold, Fred, 194
Birth, 67, 73-75, 121
  trauma, 76
Borgquist, Alvin, 20
Bowlby, John, 42-44, 108-9, 116-17,
    137 *n*
Brewster, Henry, 25-26, 113
Brodsky, Bernard, 163 *n*

Cameron, Norman, 83 *n*, 85 *n*
Castration, 76, 120-22, 160
Catharsis, 48, 50, 200
Chadwick, Mary, 160-61
Clayton, Paula, 183-86
Clergy (pastor, minister), 16, 181,
    193, 195-96, 202
Coleman, James C., 30, 137 *n*,
    138 *n*
Colitis, 114-15
Communication, 79-80, 84, 86, 90,
    112, 195, 201, 202, 209-11
Communion, 90, 202
Community, 213-14
Compensation, 105, 110, 141-42,
    144
Condemnation, 123, 155
Conditioning, 21, 87, 98, 100
Confession, 197, 209-10

Conflict(s), 64-65
Conscience, 51, 120, 125, 138
Courage, 161, 163
Creegan, Robert F., 44-45, 113-14
Crying, 97-98, 113, 183, 186

Darwin, Charles, 20
Dasein, 148, 150, 152
Death, 14, 55, 57-58, 106-7, 109,
    149-56, 159-71, 177, 207-8
  fear of, 15, 25, 50-51, 61, 96,
    102, 145-46, 157, 159-69,
    172-74, 176-77, 180
  life after, 204-5
  symbols, 169
  untimely, 45
Defense mechanisms, 105, 110-11,
    115, 117
Denial, 48, 105, 158, 160, 168, 176,
    182, 186, 200
Dependence, 23, 26-27, 68-69, 77,
    86-87, 89, 98-100, 116, 125,
    132-33, 172, 210
Depression, 30, 34, 36, 39, 43, 55-
    56, 58, 94, 107, 110, 137-40,
    144, 180, 183-84, 186-87, 189,
    196-97. *See also* Melancholia
Depressive position, 39
Despair, 20, 41, 44, 116, 123, 137
Destructiveness, 158
Detachment, 110, 138
Determinism, 164
Deutsch, Helene, 34-36, 107-8, 111,
    138 *n*, 186
Displacement, 105
Dread, 20, 37-38, 146-47, 193
Dreams, 106-7
Dying, 20, 149-50, 176

Ego
  nonpsychoanalytic, 81, 103, 107,
    112, 116, 176, 209. *See also*
    Self
  psychoanalytic, 29-32, 34, 36-43,
    56, 70-72, 76, 101-3, 108,
    120-22, 126, 129, 161-63,
    198, 201, 210

Index